Sister Sunshine

A Wartime Romance

Author's Note

The original intention was to only publish my Mum's diary. I had no intention of reading and including the letters from Tony, her future husband, but as I began to read some of them, it became clear that they should be included in this book. They are part of the story and provide a lot of detail and background. It has been an exciting but challenging exercise to blend the diary and the letters together and to allow the writing to flow. I have not included all the letters or all their details because some things need to be kept private; after all, some are indeed love letters.

I hope this will prove to be a fulfilling account of a wonderful but true story.

Dedication

To my Mum and my sister, Josephine Case.

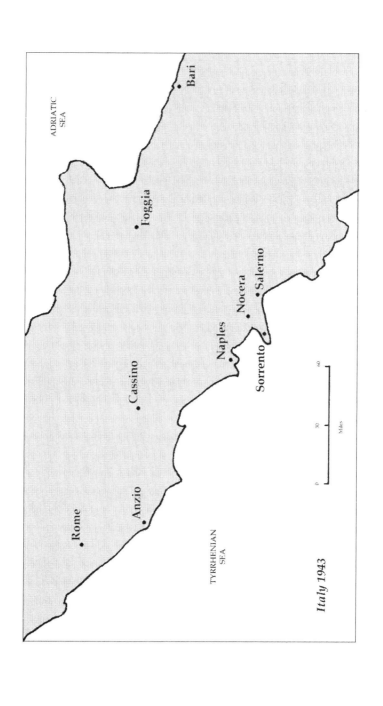

Italy 1943

Foreword

"It was pitch black outside. It should have been daylight but it wasn't. It literally rained hot ashes all day."

This was Mum's experience of the eruption of Vesuvius, my favourite story and I never tired of hearing it.

"The yard was covered in ash and when you walked across it, you could feel the heat rising up through the soles of your shoes and the smell of sulphur was awful."

We sat in the wood-panelled lounge and watched the fire in the huge grate. It crackled and threw up flames and the horse brasses on the massive beam above glinted in the firelight.

Mum sat in her brown leather chair resting her hand on the head of Angus, her Westie, her devoted little dog who faithfully followed her everywhere. As usual, she was dressed smartly in her cashmere blue jumper and tweed skirt. In her younger days Mum had stood five feet nine inches tall. Her grey curly locks used to be brown but she still had a mass of freckles up her arms. She always seemed to have a slight touch of glamour about her. My Aunt, who was also tall and very beautiful, insisted that she was half an inch taller. When they stood together people often thought they were close in age, despite the twelve year difference.

I snuggled down in my chair and waited. She gave me a little smile. "Do you really want to hear it all again?"

"Yes," I said. "I love to hear the story about Vesuvius."

It was exciting to imagine what it must have been like and I wondered if she had felt scared.

"A state of emergency was announced and we were cut off for two days and had to be dug out by the Pioneer Corps."

And so she would continue.

"I feel I'm living in a legend," is how my sister felt about Mum's stories. As children we were brought up with them. She would sit for hours and tell us all about her adventures during the Second World War. She wrote a diary and kept it by her bedside. I loved the stories and felt it was important to share them. Ordinary lives lived in exceptional situations. One can almost feel the comradeship and the excitement as well as sensing the danger and seriousness of what was going on in those years. Mum's obvious sense of humour pervades her writing, and carries the reader through.

Her diary records a brief moment in time, but what a time!

Mum was a strong character and had always been a lively, determined person. However, she was willing to laugh at life and see the funny side of things. Mum's stories were as much a part of her as everything else. They made up who she was.

Reading the diary in its entirety for the first time made quite an impact on me. All the stories that I'd grown up with and appreciated had their own individuality. Now, I have a context and that makes them all the more vivid and alive. It opened up a part of her life that I knew little about. I feel I have lived through it with her.

It is important that these memories are not forgotten and can be passed on to the next generation. Once our elderly relatives are gone, those memories and experiences are lost forever. Unless we capture them first before it is too late.

Mum was born on the 24th May, 1919. I always remember her birth year because I had a penny, in 'old money', with 1919 stamped on it. She was christened Dorothy Joyce Barber, but everyone knew her as Joy. Her parents had wanted her christened Joy but were not allowed as it was not looked upon as a 'proper' name.

She grew up in Kent and was the eldest of four children. She had two brothers and a sister. Her father owned a nursery and grew produce for Covent Garden. The house was named 'Rosedale', named after a dale found in the North York moors where her parents had spent a holiday. There were four nurseries along that particular stretch of road. The greenhouses were 200 yards long and as children it was great fun (and also very risky) to run along the narrow plank between the greenhouses. I remember doing it once. There were the packing sheds as well. Highly skilled women would carefully pack the produce. Mum remembers the drays leaving in the early hours of the morning to catch the markets. The London markets were particularly fussy. Ferns were grown all the year round and there were also tomatoes, cucumbers, lettuce, phlox and large blooms of chrysanthemum. Sometimes when there were extra flowers, bunches would be brought indoors. Their heavy scent would permeate throughout the house.

Her father had come back from the First World War a war hero. Tall, dark and handsome, he had lied about his age when he joined up so he was quite young. On one occasion the British Army needed to advance, but they had got held up by the Germans. A small group of men were needed for a very important task. He volunteered for this mission and in the dead of night went 'over the top' and cut the barbed wire fences, ready for the advance at daybreak. It was extremely dangerous. He was awarded the DCM – Distinguished Conduct Medal. He was only about eighteen.

During the Second World War he coordinated the Home Guard. As soon as the outbreak of war was announced he immediately got a shelter dug out. It was a like a trench and when the Anderson shelter was delivered in kit form, he grabbed some men from the nursery and got it assembled in the trench. My Aunt remembers steps leading down into it and a corridor and some rooms. He insisted that it must have two entrances in case one got blocked. Now my Uncle Rex had a mischievous sense of humour and put up a sign over the doorway and called it, 'The Saucy Sue'. Rex had always wanted to go to sea and at the earliest opportunity he went and joined the Merchant Navy.

In the early days of the war, fear of gas was a real danger. Granny Barber, who lived next door, would have a bath full of water set up near her shelter and would hang a wet and extremely heavy blanket across the entrance. However, it soon became apparent that gas was not going to be a danger.

Mum remembers a picture of Vesuvius hanging on the wall at her Granny's house. Granny Barber's sitting room was at the front of the house and was seldom used, except for special occasions. The picture of Vesuvius hung there and it had always fascinated Mum. Little did she know that one day she would see the volcano for real and be caught up in its devastating power.

During the war, Mum joined the Queen Alexandra Imperial Military Nursing Service, known as The QAs. Nursing required at least three years of training which she started at the Kent & Sussex Hospital, Royal Tunbridge Wells. The training was hard and nurses were expected to work long hours and they got very little time off. They were not allowed to marry during training. If a nurse wanted to get married she had to leave. It was as simple as that. Matrons in those days were formidable and ruled with a rod of iron. The discipline was very strict and not for the faint hearted.

Mum must have looked very smart in her crisp nurses' uniform, black stockings, stripped dress and starched white apron. She wore a stiff white collar buttoned tightly around her neck and a white cap would sit on her brown curly hair. Under her chin was a neat white bow. On the apron was pinned the Kent and Sussex Hospital badge. The bold, blue lettering stood out against the silver background. In the middle were the red, yellow and blue emblems of the hospital and underneath were the words, 'Do well doubt not.'

In 1942, she joined the QAs and was posted to Leeds Castle near Maidstone. Her second posting was at Netley Hospital.

Her posting overseas was with the 103 Hospital and they would set up field hospitals behind the 1st Army lines in North Africa. Later, she was sent to Italy. She was often referred to as, 'Sister Sunshine', because she was always cheerful and smiling.

She met Tony Case, who was to be my sister's father, whilst working on the wards in England. He was a patient with a broken leg caused by a motorbike accident. He was a lively patient and she was warned to 'take care' by his interfering father!

Tony had decided on a career in the army when he was seventeen. His father had been a Captain during the First World War. Tony joined The Sherwood Foresters and would later see much action in North Africa and Italy. At the time of going abroad he had the rank of Lieutenant. He was twenty years old.

The following are extracts from Mum's personal diary. Some of the details are stories that she told to me, and some are taken from her diary.

This is her story

England 1942

Summer

Doing Sister Holiday Relief on Men's Surgical Ward, No 1 General, No 2 Officers' Ward. Tony patient with broken leg from motor bike accident.

Back in theatre. Visits from Tony – on crutches! Persistent young man. Have to admit, very attractive. Tony discharged to convalesce. Visits continue and becoming serious.

Tony back with his Unit stationed locally. Frequent meetings – Sevenoaks – London. Even took him home to meet the family. Whoops!

Matron offered me post of Sister on ENT (ear nose and throat) wards and theatre but had already decided to volunteer for Military Service.

November

Joined Queen Alexandra's Imperial Military Nursing Service, Reserves (QAIMNS/R). First posting, Leeds Castle near Maidstone, an Officers' hospital.

Leeds Castle

Living in a castle quite an experience. Part supposedly haunted. Very noisy at night due to the peacocks! Beyond the drawbridge, a sentry on duty – to ward off intruders?! My friend Scotty convinced some ghosts thereabouts in the ruins beyond the moat.

Leeds Castle was owned by Lady Baillie. She had bought it in 1926 and it was converted to a hospital during the early part of the war. Mum felt she was sent there to learn how to be in the army and to understand how the army worked. She was also given a rank.

State registered nurses working in the armed forces were awarded Commissioned Office status in 1941. As Mum was a Sister her rank was Lieutenant and so she would have been saluted by the lower ranks.

She had her nursing duties but she said there was also an awful lot of paperwork. Fortunately, she was given a couple of orderlies who would do it for her. Staff Sergeant Skinner worked with Mum for the whole duration of her time in the army and he was in charge of all the orderlies.

Unaware had an admirer – Tank Reg Padre visiting the sick. Patients joked it was me, not them, he came to see! Finally accepted Padre's invitation to dinner, Maidstone Hotel. My carriage was what appeared to be a baby tank! (later told a scout car). Embarrassed to have a proposal of marriage – oh dear! Said I was already engaged – sort of!
Tony very attentive, am much attracted – is this love?!

Weekend leave with Tony in London.

Saw 'Road to Morocco' starring Bob Hope and Bing Crosby. We decided to make part of the film our 'code' to know where we were as I also would shortly be going overseas. Was three months at Leeds Castle.

Second posting to Netley Hospital.

Mobilising for Overseas Service began. Not issued with tropical kit so we think North Africa. Tony already there.

Mum and Tony were already an item at this point. She literally follows her true love over the sea.

There is another voice in this story, the voice of Tony her fiancée and future husband. Tony's letters give us a lot of insight into the life and thoughts of a young man, a soldier, often in dangerous places and situations. The one thing that helps him get through it is his love for Joy.

All the letters that passed between Joy and Tony had to go through the censor. This means that every letter was read by a third party. One of the reasons for this was to make sure that if the letters happened to fall into enemy hands, no vital information could be given away. Each envelope was stamped with the censor seal and on top were the words, 'On Active Service'. It feels quite poignant to open these letters and read the contents which are often hastily scribbled down in pen or pencil. Sometimes his letters contain some colourful language as one would expect from a soldier!

Tony Case

Staff-Nurse, Kent and Sussex Hospital 1942

Frederick Barber senior 1918

1943

January

Joy my own,

For three days we had rather rough weather, and the old ship nearly stood on her head. I haven't been ill yet but about sixty per cent of the troops were just about prostrate. They really are the most wonderful people I ever hope to meet. Quite frankly they are very uncomfortable – very crowded and the food is not at all good. The bad weather on top of all that made their situation almost unbearable. But they put up with it like the grand fellows they are. Of course they grumbled a bit – who wouldn't? But, I am in the uncomfortable position of having to censor my platoon's letters, and their cheerfulness when they write home amazes me. When we left the port they cheered and sang like mad – it was more than I could do. I'm terribly proud of them, and I feel very honoured that I have the privilege to go abroad with them.

Your photograph hangs at the bottom of my bed and I just lie and gaze at it until I fall asleep – and then it's the first thing I see when I wake up. It's a queer state of affairs. I feel so sad, and yet I like feeling that way.

Every night we have been giving a concert party to entertain the lads. I was in a sketch entirely done by Officers and of course I had the part of 'Little Nell' - Don't you dare laugh.

10th January

I expect that you'll have guessed by now that we're in North Africa. Of course I can't tell you exactly where we are, but we're all quite safe and sound. The trip over here was uneventful and if I hadn't been leaving you behind, it might have been quite pleasant.

My impressions of this place are a vague sort of jumble of filthy Arabs, talkative Frenchmen, and bags of oranges, tangerines, lemons and dates. There's a strange mixture of beauty and indescribable filth all mixed up so that you can't distinguish the one from the other. We are about fourteen miles from the city and there is quite a lot of fun to be had there in one way or another. Mostly one way, I fear, which means that we drink a hell of a lot of wine. Who wouldn't with champagne at one shilling a glass?

The weather is very like late spring in England, warm days and cold nights. There is snow on the hills, and people coming back from the front tell us that the chief difficulty is keeping warm. The country side is similar to England, except for the orange groves, palms, cactuses and acres of vine fields. It could be very beautiful, but the squalor spoils it all.

We are only about four miles away from the General Hospital, and Colonel Martin invites us over to tea at the Sisters' Mess occasionally. It makes me very homesick and melancholy to see all those girls with their QA badges. Poor kids, they were sunk on the way over and all their kit was lost so they are wearing khaki battledress, but managing to keep fairly cheerful.

Keep on writing to me darling. I'm hoping for a colossal mail when it eventually does arrive.

8th February

My dearest,

If you could only know just how much your letters have helped me. As long as I can have some connection with you – however remote it may be – then I shall be alright. We have recently been given permission to say that we are at the front. I hope that will excuse my not writing more often. Shortage of paper is only one of the many difficulties attached to letter writing here. I've just about purged my soul in scrounging these few sheets.

On the whole, life is pretty bloody awful. For the last few days we've been up to our knees in mud. I haven't had a wash or shave for forty eight hours so I should imagine that I look a pretty ghastly mess too. In fact I don't think you'd own me if you could see me now. But I'm keeping fit. The food keeps coming along nicely, and damn good it is too. I think I could make some of the people back in England quite envious. Really, apart from the weather and other quite unavoidable discomforts, we haven't got a lot to complain about.

It's rather queer writing to you and not knowing exactly where you are. If you are following in the footsteps of Bing Crosby and Bob Hope then at least you'll be in the same continent as me. Because you're glad that you're coming abroad then I'm glad too. But Joy, my dear heart, it's no use pretending that I'm not worried.

15th February

Joy my own,

How I wish I could know exactly where you are. I'm terribly glad to know that at last you're happy and that you're going to have the opportunity of doing what you've wanted to do. I'm terribly proud of you darling for being so eager to get into the middle of it all. On the other hand, I'd give all I have to know right now that you're safe and well.

It's amazing the changes a life like this can make in a man. For instance, up 'til now, I would have gone through my life just waiting for things to happen and then dealing with the situation as it arises. Now I have become a creature of premonitions. And I'm learning to rely on my instinct. Once already it has definitely saved my life. I'll tell you about it one day.

We're all in the best of spirits out here. There's a rumour of some more mail on the way and the excitement amongst the lads is colossal. It's almost pitiful to watch the way they positively devour their letters. I always have to wait until I am quite alone before I dare open mine in case I should make a fool of myself.

I'm in disgustingly good health and I'm actually putting on weight – though not through lack of exercise I assure you. But the food is damn good. There we are at the front, shells whistling in all directions and this morning I had for breakfast two delicious sausages and a couple of fried eggs. So after that meal, the first wash for three days and the first shave for five, I'm feeling more like The Lieutenant R A Case of The Sherwood

Foresters, and less like the tired, dishevelled mud-covered individual I was three hours ago. There's not much glamour or glory about all this. In fact it's rather a monotonous routine of hard work by night and a few snatched hours of rest by day.

I belong to you Joy, all of me. I shall always love you. Tony

Now back to the diary.

13th March

Arrived in the middle of the night in blackout train at Avonmouth, Bristol. Sailed on a hospital ship called HMHS Newfoundland.
As we left the docks were cheered on our way by dockers. Only twelve QAs on board.
Because of mine fields in the Bristol Channel, sailed round the top of Ireland, into the teeth of a force ten gale.
Busy destroyer warning us off convoy.

They would be given their orders and were not told where they were going as it was all top secret and must have been rather exciting, or scary, or both. The blackout train would have had its blinds down. Any city they passed through would also be in total darkness.

At one time when I was a young girl, we were travelling towards London in the car at night and Mum pointed out the glow in the sky.

"During the war, you wouldn't have seen that," she told me and that had always stuck in my mind.

In the evening, the blackout train arrived at Avonmouth. The hospital ship that they boarded happened to be the very same ship that Mum's cousin, Charles Antlett, had been on as a scout when he sailed to Australia. The HMHS Newfoundland was later torpedoed near Salerno during the invasion.

Hospital ships needed to be clearly identified as such because attacking one was considered a war crime. Large red crosses would be painted on the sides and at night they had to be clearly visible. Mum told me that their ship was all lit-up like a Christmas tree. However, it kept getting mixed up with the convoy as they had trouble controlling the now-empty ship. A small destroyer kept signalling them to keep away because the convoy was meant to be travelling in total darkness. It was such a rough sea that the little destroyer kept disappearing in the deep troughs of the waves only to reappear again still flashing its message.

Gibraltar

18th March Gibraltar

The Rock looked sheer & impressive and bristling with unseen guns. The bay was filled with navy shipping of every kind; Rodney, Nelson, Battleships, Destroyers and Corvettes…
Vivid blue sky and sea, blazing sunshine, multi-coloured distant hills – abundance of wild spring flowers and … BANANAS!! Small boats buzzing around offering them to us, not seen at home for four years.

Evening

Myriads of lights shining on The Rock and across the water in Spanish Morocco.

Night

We are anchored in this harbour surrounded by other ships of the navy. Black velvet sky, the swish of water against the side of the ship – safe after our violent journey, through the Bay of Biscay, calm after the storm.

19th March Morning

Such a welcome, invitations galore to visit other ships – Matron unwilling to let us go! However, some high up Naval Commander persuaded her we would be safe!!! Parties ++, men, men and more men – but we must be properly escorted by Naval Officers! Laughter and fun.
Held up for 2 weeks because of U-boat activity in the Med. A large convoy had been attacked.

There were QAs stationed permanently at Gibraltar, but people rarely saw them. It was a standing joke that they were afraid to come out because of all the men! There were very few females so Mum and the other nurses would have had numerous invitations to visit the ships.

"It was the first time I tasted rum!" she confessed to me once.

Poor Little Patience

Mum had told me about a time when she was attending lip-reading classes in Wells. She said that she had made quite a few friends, one of them being Frances, who made her laugh a lot and had a terrific sense of humour.

Most of the class were of a particular age and had lived through the war years. One day, Mum was sitting between 'poor little Patience', who was 81, three years younger than herself, and Frances.

Apparently, Patience had been a Wren during the war and was sent to Gibraltar.

"I was sent to Gibraltar in 1943. When were you there?" Mum asks her.

"1944," says Patience.

"Did you enjoy it?"

"Oh no," says Patience. "It was awful," she says with a very straight face. "I was only 18, and my parents hadn't told me anything."

Mum said that she was aware of Frances gently shaking with suppressed laughter at her side. She had told me that Patience was a vicar's daughter and had clearly led a sheltered life. She said Patience had continued with the same very straight face, talking about the men. Here, Mum searches for Patience's exact words.

"They wanted so much."

At this point, Frances couldn't contain herself any longer and burst out laughing.

When I asked Mum about her time in Gibraltar she had replied, "I had the time of my life. It was marvellous."

But I add not in that sort of way, it was the social life that Mum enjoyed.

North Africa

28th March

Sailed up the med to Algiers. Sad farewell beneath the stars. From the deck watched the twinkling lights of Gibraltar disappear. Sunny peaceful days in the Med, lay on the deck all day eating oranges and almonds. One Jerry plane came and took a look at us. It was announced that everyone was to go up on deck so that the plane could see nurses etc. were on board. Red crosses ablaze. He went away – bit scary though.

31st March Algiers

Dazzling white buildings shining in the morning sun. Palm trees.
Our men, doctors and orderlies welcoming us at the dockside but they were dressed in odds & ends, and looked a real mess, a bit untidy!
"Is this how you dress for active service?" someone called out. The answer that came back was that they had been torpedoed, and lost most of their gear. Only one orderly was lost. A lot of equipment had been lost including the Padre's record collection.

Journey to Guyotville

Guyotville, seaside 'playground' for the French families living in Algiers – expense no object judging by the luxury surroundings – now taken over by the British Army!
Our men go ahead to find suitable area for field hospital. Sisters went to Transit Camp. Dusty white road. Arabs in picturesque ragged costumes, brilliant colours and bearded (rather frightening) faces, filthy barefooted children, veiled cowed women.

Transit camp

Gay, luxury white villas on a headland, rocky, beautiful coastline, brilliant blue sea, white crested waves breaking at our feet.
Tent for our 'Mess' - our first taste of canvas living! Using our camp kit in empty villas, trouble with beds! Fortunately our batmen dealt with this problem.
Sort of holiday – lazed on the rocks and silver sand in next bay.

Tony is wounded in the Tunisian Campaign and gets packed off to the 5th General Hospital. He has to be operated on and have two pieces of shell removed, one from his foot and one from his side. He tells Joy not to worry about him and he remarks about the Sisters.

The Sisters are all old and ugly and their uniforms don't fit. Oh what memories the sight of the grey and red bring back.

He gets moved to the 94th General Hospital. Mum quickly receives news about him.

3rd April

Dispatch rider brought message – Tony wounded and in 94th G Base Hospital in Algiers! Amid great excitement, Frances and I hitched a lift in army jeep to Algiers and out to Beni Messous – became daily occurrence, starting after breakfast, returning for supper.

Tony suggests we get married!! Wow, I am staggered – could we? How? Apply for permission to marry from our Colonels. I have to tell and ask Miss Blore (Matron). She's shocked and not very helpful. However Colonel delighted. Some holdup, question asked in Houses of Parliament, North Africa being a foreign country and a war zone. Tony said he'd get it sorted. Then was told he was to be evacuated to UK. 'No way!' said he. Hectic two days getting it cancelled!

Getting a Licence

Getting married appears to be a bit of a procedure.

They had to get written permission from both their COs and then had to apply for a licence.

Tony's Letter

Joy, my darling,
Not very good news today I'm afraid. The Padre tells me that the authorities have not yet decided what is to be done about British marriages out here. So it looks as though we shall just have to wait until they can make up their minds. It's infuriating, but nothing will hurry them. We shall just have to be patient a little longer. Go ahead. My sweet one, and send me that authorisation from your CO or whatever he is. Then when the time comes, there will be no delay.

He tries to find information about other marriages that have taken place in North Africa as his Commandant feels that specific names and details would help.

The old boy says that it would be useful if we could quote definite instances of marriages out here.

Tony also finds newspaper cuttings about people who have been married in Cairo. He gives these to the Commandant who will use them in evidence on their behalf. The Senior Chaplain has a folder full of letters and notes about Tony and Joy and he does all he can to help the young couple. The Chaplain's advice is to wait for the GRO.

Eventually Tony finds out that the GRO will cover every kind of marriage and a whole heap of arrangements have to be made with the French Government.

His letters become more frequent and a feeling of urgency creeps in. At one point, it's all looking a bit precarious and uncertain. He writes again.

I've a horrid feeling that something big is going to start very soon and then who knows what will happen? I may get whisked off to Europe or on the other hand you may be so busy that they can't spare you when the time comes for us to get married. Afraid I'm being an awful little pessimist. Sorry!

He continues to sort out all the arrangements while he is convalescing.

Meanwhile, Mum travels inland to the site where the Field Hospital will be set up.

15th April Leave for Mecha Chateaudun

Terrible train journey, thirty six hours through mountainous desert country, no sign of life, bleak and barren. Intense heat, flies and dust. Black smuts from engine – shortage of water. Slept! On stretchers, choked by smoke, bumped and bruised.
Arrived exhausted, filthy and thirsty! Ambulances race train to station, loud cheers as we climb down – our workmates, doctors and orderlies very pleased to see us and anxious to make us welcome.

Darkness falling, bumpy ride to hospital – immense rocky field, SAND! planted with tents – rocky, semi-mountainous hills around, no trees, no other sign of vegetation – could be the surface of the moon?? Where are we? Apparently on a plateau, some miles from Constantine. Bitterly cold nights despite intense daytime heat.

WORK next morning equipping wards – four large, twenty four-bedded tents. Me as Medical 1 with Capt. Brod and four orderlies plus one Staff Sgt. and two clerks (privates), to help with clerical work and keeping general good order! Fortunately they all took to their female 'boss' with good humour! Capt. Brod, my boss, was Czechoslovakian.

No patients yet – our side not very busy.

Living Quarters

Sisters' lines somewhat removed from male staff lines?! We have large Mess tent equipped with own chef and batmen/orderlies. Our sleeping tents are IPs Indian Pattern – in two lines, and we share two to a tent. The loos are on the far horizon or so it seems if you're in a hurry! four seated per side with canvas screens between the 'holes'! Food pretty basic and in short supply – I like corned beef!

Living under canvas put Mum off camping for life and hence when I was a child, we never went camping.

The Field Hospital, No 103, sited close to the railway line, single track, with passing spaces, which runs across top of North Africa, hugging coast few miles inland. Patients boarded on ambulance train from Front Line Dressing Station. Our hospital is half-way to Base Hospital, Algiers. Our job, as train stops at holt close by, was to take off the more urgent cases for treatment – others went on to Base.

Slight hitch before we could start taking patients… sudden tropical RAIN – duration three weeks! Colonel had been informed that rainy season over! Ho! Ho! Camp awash with slippery sandy mud. Colonel puts us into <u>male</u> *battledress and army boots – quite lethal – I fell into a ditch (helpfully dug by RE (Royal Engineer) unit to drain the camp site).*

Throughout her life Mum was never comfortable wearing trousers. I remember she did not approve of my sister and I wearing trousers into town but, that soon changed. She was, after all, of a generation that felt you were not properly dressed unless you had matching shoes, handbag and gloves.

I was rescued by my Staff Sgt. Skinner – very wet, muddy and terrified – I want to go home! This life not for me – seems I have fallen at the 1st hurdle! However, with great care, taken into the Clerk's tent and plied with very strong sweet tea – cure for all ills in a sticky situation. Staff Sgt. Skinner forty years +, regular army, deemed too old for fighting unit, transferred to RAMC (Royal Army Medical Corps).

As such, knows full well how to cope when stationed in wild and unfriendly situations.

Brewing up...

British Army – salt of the Earth. Interesting how they 'Brew Up' as it's called.
Washed out petrol can.
Packet or two STRONG TEA.
Milk – condensed
Water to fill can.
Fire. Gather stones to make fireplace – set alight. Bob's your Uncle! The result in my case simply foul, but I had to accept their concern for me, and their kindness with good grace, and profuse thanks. I think we will make a good team.

My Nursing Orderlies also friendly and fairly well trained in Basic Nursing. GDO (General Duty Orderly) *bottom of the pack – empty the slops and bins, carry water containers from the Cook House – you name it. My GDO named Bailly. We have been in action for a while now, large numbers of acute cases. Prepare large tent ward in hurry, all hands on deck – grabbed Bailly, although not a Nursing Orderly – could teach him as we go along – no need, he knew. Why? He said he had been a hospital porter!*
"Why didn't you tell them?"
"They didn't ask!"
Must get him to take the training exams on offer – will increase his pay and allowance to his wife. He

was chuffed, said he'd like that.
Tony still at convalescent hospital, daily letters –
very chirpy.

He would write almost daily and sometimes twice a day. He longs for Joy's letters and she in turn longs for his. The post was not always reliable and often letters would arrive in batches, sometimes months later. He admits that he would carry about six of her letters wherever he went and read them again and again. While they are apart, the letters provided him a way of feeling close to her. He describes them as the one bright part of rather gloomy days.

20th April

Dearest Heart,
This letter is written to you by kind permission of the German High Command. What I really mean is that I 'borrowed' this paper off a Hun. Poor kid, he was only about eighteen – and so scared I think he'd have given me his trousers if I'd asked for them.
I'm getting terribly browned off with this place. Have taken to gambling the last two evenings with disastrous results. Shall have to give it up soon or I shan't have enough to get married with. There was a concert yesterday evening – all male and all British and really very good. It was held in the medical block which is a building built in a square with terraces around a very pleasant courtyard. The audience sat on the steps of the

terraces and the artists performed in the courtyard underneath the stars. I got very sentimental – it's remarkable what a pleasant noise a whole lot of soldiers can make when they sing softly.

I think I'm missing you more than ever before if that is possible. Darling I hope that you're happy at your new place. I'm afraid you'll find it very strange and probably very hard work. But when you realise how grateful the boys are to you for just being out here (they are, even if they don't show it) I'm sure you'll think it worthwhile. Just remember that I love you with all my heart and soul. Tony

24th April Tony's comment on Joy's hospital

Had a glorious letter from you today, consequently the sun is shining again. I was rather afraid that you might get a bit of a shock when you saw the hospital – they certainly seem to have given you rather a dirty deal. Never mind dearest one, I'm sure you'll soon realise how grateful we all are to you. We censor the patients' letters here, and have done in all the other hospitals, and they have nothing but praise for you.
When you're feeling low, just think of the marvellous things in store for us. I always do and it works wonders.

1st May

We arrived here yesterday. For a change, I think I shall be able to write a fairly interesting letter. Let me start with the journey down here. There were eighteen of us *from the 94th and we rode in a large troop–carrier, much to everybody's amusement.*

We hadn't been on the way more than ten minutes when we persuaded the driver to stop at a café. Four of us got together and in about twenty minutes we had knocked back four bottles of champagne. A good start, you might say. After about another forty minutes or so, we had to stop in a town to ask the way, and there the process was repeated.

Eventually we arrived at about 4 o'clock, semi pickled and in grand form. To our delight we found that there was a bar on the premises. In we trooped, and as I can remember, there we stayed until midnight. The net result is that today I have the prince of all hangovers.

This really is a delightful place. It's a little village right on the shore underneath three very large and beautiful mountains. The trees and grass grow right down to the beach and there are some marvellous sands, rocks and cliffs.

The army has taken over the biggest and best hotel in the place, complete, and turned it into a Convalescent Home for Officers. The staff consists of Le Patron, Madame, another woman of sorts, three assorted waiters, thirty odd soldiers (batmen) and a cook. The place was only started the day before yesterday and as yet we are a bit disorganised. But soon it will be just grand. The food is rather French – but good. The only snag is that we're more than fifty miles west of Algiers. But there is a small amount of transport and I have fixed up a trip to Algiers for early next week.

Oh my dearest heart, I wish you could be with me. I'm sure you'd love this place. The village consists mainly of bungalows and villas on the shore. There is one other hotel, as yet untouched by the army, but nevertheless very well tried out already. We are the first British troops they have seen.

Darling, you were paid the prettiest complement yesterday. We were talking about French girls (subject normal) and one chap in the Irish Guards made quite a long speech, the gist of which was as follows.

"Of course young Tony here is the luckiest bloke (or words to that effect) in this army. The prettiest girl I've seen arrives in the hospital, and just as I'm getting all excited about it, in steps Case. I notice that she's wearing a ring, and discover that they're going to get married out here. Too bloody bad."

Oh Darling, I'm so proud of you. I wonder if I really deserve you. I'm determined that whatever happens I shall see you again soon. I'm to have my plaster off on the 15th of this month. After that – well be prepared for anything.

4th May Bathing Beauties

At last the weather has improved. Glorious sunshine all day. The sunshine has brought out the local inhabitants. Great excitement amongst us here at the appearance of quite a bevy of bathing beauties. It really was quite amusing to see about sixty hungry looking Officers goggling at about half a dozen wenches and trying to think of the French for, "What about having a drink with me tonight?

26th May Hell

Joy, my own,
There was a new intake of Officers today, and among
them were three people I knew very well. One is from
my own Battalion, another is a lad from Derby in the
2nd Foresters, and the third is a chap whom I was at
school with and whom I haven't seen since. As you can
imagine there's quite a considerable party going on that
we're going to have together.

Thank you for giving me something to live for, to
hold on to, and to fight for. In fact – for everything. The
more convinced I am that every man – Jack, who has
come out of that hell with a sane mind, must have had
somebody or something to hang on to, to keep them
going. As far as I was concerned, it was you. I love
Britain and I love my home – yes. But, darling one, I
love you far more.

I have excused myself for a few minutes to write to
you. I don't really want to have a party. I don't really
enjoy getting tight. All I want is you. All of you – and
forever.

Yet another letter from you this evening. Dearest
heart, I'm so grateful to you. Not only for your letters,
but for everything. For giving me a reason for my life –
in fact for making my life worthwhile. For all the
happiness you've given me. Perhaps you will realise
now just how much marrying you will mean to me.

I must stop now. I am being called, shouted at and
was sworn at, from the doorway of the bar.
All my love, Joy, dear one. From Tony

6th June

Your letter arrived in the middle of a colossal party. I was being rather a wet blanket I fear, having retired into a corner and read your letter about six times. I let out a loud whoop, plunged into the bar and didn't emerge again except to take part in an extremely boisterous glide into which I was press-ganged. If I don't have to go and explain myself to the Commandant again in the morning, I shall be a very lucky bloke.

Bags of Sisters arrived today and as far as I can gather everything was very successful. We've got hold of a very good army band. It really looked rather delightful to see the white uniforms and khaki dancing together on the veranda.

10th June

Joy darling,
After I'd written to you last night – I'd worked myself into such a mood that I just couldn't go to bed. So I went for a stroll. On my way – met a pal of mine – he's in love too – who was mooning about looking lost. So we decided we'd go for a bathe. It was just as marvellous as anything can be when you're not with me. A warm night, a calm sea, a glorious moon and thousands of stars. When we swam, hundreds of little sparks glittered in the water. It was all so beautiful and I wished so much that you could have been with me.

Thursday 24th June

Joy, dearest one,
Have just got back from Algiers – I'm absolutely dead beat. If I don't go to bed soon I shall fall asleep here. The drive back here in an ambulance is just about the world's worst. Haven't enjoyed myself a bit. Algiers is the hottest, dustiest, dirtiest, most expensive, smelliest town I ever wish to visit. Slept on the ship for a short time and also had a trip around the harbour this morning.

The diary also refers to the scorching heat and the palpable dryness of the place.

June

Days of intense heat, but nights very cold. Blazing relentless sun, no shade, bare rock, no green, nothing grows!
Sirocco fierce wind blowing off the desert, sand storms every day – sand everywhere, eat it, drink it, in our clothes, in our beds! The sand gets into everything and sticks to you. The wind drops with sundown, but is there again in the morning.

Constantine

Small party, Doctors, Sisters got together and arranged trip to Constantine in borrowed

ambulance! Amazing city built by the Romans on two mountain tops – bridges connecting the two sections.
Meal in Officers' Mess – sort of palace taken over by the army.

Night Duty

Different team, but find I still have my Senior Nursing Orderly and Bailly – appears they asked for the move to stay in my team. Sleep very difficult, dust, flies, lizards. We sleep NUDE under our mosquito nets. Our Batmen bang noisily on our tent poles to wake us up before appearing with our tea! Time to grab a sheet.

Fire

Sgt. Major organised group to burn dried up vegetation (fire hazard) around camp, presumably to create a fire barrier! Went wrong, got out of control, caught alight the last tent in our night staff lines. Shouting woke me up – mine 3rd tent down, able to get out and collapse it, a method we had been shown to do in such an emergency – grabbed clothes and RAN! Amazed to find Tony had arrived, and outside our Mess in some panic! Draped in a sheet, covered in sweat and sand – assured him I am OK, except for blisters on hands. The fire under control, two tents totally lost, and four girls lost all their kit. United with my trusty tin trunk. RSM for Court Marshal!

Tony had flown up from Algiers, able to stay weekend. Blissful.

Day Duty

Back with Capt. Brod, my old team and faithful Bailly, now happily getting upgraded to Nursing Orderly 2nd class.

I love the way Bailly features in Mum's diary. He was often there in the background, helping out and giving support. She claimed that he was not her batman but he often took on the role of one. She always spoke very highly of him and they obviously made a good team.

Another duty that Captain Brod had to carry out was assessing certain men who were showing signs of mental stress or unusual behaviour and whether they were fit enough to be returned to the front. There was the story of the man who claimed he had an imaginary dog. Another man would insist on putting out the hymn books in the chapel and then carefully and methodically collect them all in again. He would do this every day whether there was a service or not. We do not know what happened to these individuals and I am sure there were more that have not been mentioned.

At last, the letter she has been waiting for arrives on the 16th July.

Sweetheart mine,

It's all fixed Joy darling. You're very nearly Mrs. Case. Went into Algiers and saw the Consul, bought the licence and arranged the whole thing. We can get married any time after the 28th of this month.

I've been in Algiers two days which accounts for there being no letters. The trouble was I was so excited about it all that I told the whole story to a bunch of complete strangers in the Officers' Club. They thought it was a whale of a show and insisted that I had my bachelor party there and then – which I did, with no little success.

So there we are, dearest heart. Goodnight, my dear one. I shall always love you. Tony

It has taken three months to get the permission in place and make all the arrangements. Work continues as usual at the Field Hospital.

Malaria season and dysentery. Working hard, two divisions, two hundred patients. Strong winds – sand storms every day.
Two more flying visits from Tony. Wedding arrangements settled!! My leave arranged, given my travel warrant and the blessings of my Colonel. Feeling very excited and can hardly believe this is going to happen.

30th July

Board 'Rapide'(plush 1st class carriage) for Algiers. Misnomer, not really fast at all, except that it does the journey in one day. Single track but at intervals, passing places. Hectic, sweaty journey, in company with four other male Officers (not from our unit). Arrive <u>four hours late</u>. Frantic Tony on platform. Happy, happy reunion.

31st July

Married in the British Consulate by the Consul, also had religious marriage service in English Church in Algiers. Had spent the night (alone) in strange 'Arabian Nights' type hotel. Got lost trying to find a restaurant for breakfast. Tony arrived early to rescue me with taxi, off to the Consulate, driven by a hunchback.   – Could be lucky –
Carved splendid marble staircase, hand in hand and laughing happily, ascended. We forgot needed two witnesses! The Consul greeted us and laughed at our lack of insight, and summoned two clerks to do the job! An official piece of paper declaring us truly married. Congratulations all round and many good wishes.
Off in same taxi to the English Church.

English Church

Here met by various friends Tony has accumulated while being in hospital and convalescing – good at this sort of thing. Fatherly Maj. Lynn Harris to give me away and Tony's Captain friend to be the best man. Huge bouquet of flowers.

Reception

Reception in apartment owned by Viscount Corvedale, Tony met him in Officers' Club, heard of forth coming marriage, and insisted on playing host to celebrations. Large gathering, a few QAs from 94th Base Hospital – didn't know a soul. Champagne ++ photos, silly speeches! Great fun.
Left for luncheon - wedding breakfast. Party of ten guests. I was the only woman – can't remember what we ate! We slip away quietly, and wander around the town in something of a haze, and thinking we were on cloud nine.

Honeymoon in Chenoua Plage

Nine days heaven in almost paradise! We arrived in time for dinner, followed by a dance. Lt. Col. in charge arranged a big celebration party including getting an orchestra. Convalesced patients, Doctors, Sisters, all known to Tony, or most of them. I was overwhelmed.

Whenever it was seen that we were dancing together, the orchestra played the Anniversary Waltz.

This was a beautiful French holiday resort – white villas, blue and green shutters. Verandahs covered in vines, colourful creepers, shady trees, figs – rocky beautiful coastline, golden sands. Moonlight bathing in the cove. Introduced to playing poker! Some French still here, a café still functioning. Dinner under the trees, café on the cliff. Watched big yellow moon rise out of the sea. Hitched one trip into Algiers, looked at the shops – pretty bare. Casbah out of bounds – looked and smelled interesting. Pity not allowed in.

8th August

End of holiday. Back to Algiers for one day. Went to a sort of night club, naval types all over the place – several Destroyers in harbour, invited onto one of them for hectic party – their relaxation between sorties in the Med.

9th August

Up at 6.30am to catch 'Rapide'. Travel together, me to 103, Tony back to his unit somewhere on front line. Sad journey back. We got very dirty from soot, very hot and tired. Slept most of the way. Bailed out at 103 General Hospital. Tony put up in Officers' Mess for night – not allowed to be with me!

10th August

Tony goes off to join his unit, me, duty on Med Ward. More Sirocco, heat and flies. Work ++

German Patients

Back with Capt. Brod. again. Influx of Prisoners of War – our division had to take the Germans as Brod only doctor to speak German. They are well behaved, but surly. Some fighting amongst themselves, so Brod separated the non-Nazis from the more militant types.

Day Duty

After the American Air Force arrive, there was one particular German patient who would look under the folded-back tent walls and count the American 'Flying Fortresses' going out in the morning. He would take great delight in counting them when they came back, to see if any were missing.
Some of the Germans very aggressive, and maintain they will win the war!

Night Duty

Two wards of prisoners. Only one sentry – rather frightening. However, no trouble.

September

RATD arrive! Royal Artillery Training Depot. Tented camp almost on our doorstep. Hostilities over in North Africa, easing of restrictions, fewer patients, mostly medical.

Our chef prides himself on his ability with low and uninteresting rations, and with Matron's permission, would like to serve old fashioned 'Afternoon Teas' on Sundays. We thought it a great idea and it worked. So successful, word got about, not only our own Officers begging for an invitation, but somehow the news got to the RA Depot. Every Sunday our Mess was the most popular place on the planet!

A Visitor

I was writing up notes in my office tent when a young Sgt. came in. I didn't look up.

"Yes?" I said.

He didn't say anything and just stood there. When I finally looked up, all I could see was this huge grin under his cap. Heavens! It's Freddie! (one of Mum's brothers). He was with the 8th Army but fighting was over. He hitched through the 1st Army lines searching for the 103 hospital and found me. We collapsed in laughter and embraces. We had two happy days talking, talking!!

Mum and Freddie were very close in age. They did everything together when they were younger and most people thought they were twins.

Freddie moved to Australia to live when he was older and came to visit England in 2014 (the first time he had been back to the country in over two decades). Like Mum, he is full of stories. Freddie was busy chatting away to various members of the family in another part of the house, when I remember my cousin coming into the room and exclaiming, "Dad's on about the war again!"

He told me a lot about his childhood and some of the things, he and Mum would get up to. This is just one of those things:

The Clock Incident

Mother and Father played tennis. They would leave Joy in charge of brother Rex, who would only have been a small child at the time. Granny, who lived next door, would bang on the kitchen wall if the kids got too noisy. One game Freddie & Joy would play was 'chasing'. This involved opening a window downstairs and the two windows onto the balcony. It wasn't a real balcony as there were no doors, a 'show piece' as Freddie called it. The kids would climb in and out of the windows, much to the alarm of the neighbour across the road, who could see all this happening!

Sometimes, Rex would get in the way until his bed time at 7 o'clock, so they would try to put him to bed earlier. The problem was that Father had taught him how to read the Roman numerals on the clock and he would point at the clock and say, "But it's not 7 o'clock yet!"

So Joy and Freddie came up with a plan. Joy would take Rex out of the room on some false pretence leaving Freddie to climb up and change the hands on the clock. When Rex was safely in bed Freddie would then have to put the hands back to the right time, but he didn't always get it right. Years and years later the truth came out.

"I wondered why that clock was playing up!" said Father.

Chatting to Freddie, I asked him if he had ever smoked, this was his reply,

"I gave it up when I was nine years old!" he said with a twinkle in his eye. "I tried one of Father's pipes and didn't like it!"

Freddie loved horses and would spend hours down at the local stables. When he signed up to fight, he wanted to join the Cavalry.

"Sorry mate," he was told. "No cavalry in this war!"

So he joined the artillery instead.

ENSA Concert

Rather rude – but went down well with the patients and our male staff.

Two women from YMCA arrived to cheer us all up! They persuaded the REs to erect canvas screens around small area of tables and chairs creating what we are pleased to call the 'Hula Hula' and these two wonderful ladies produced 'teas', scones and things but mainly wonderful dishes with melon which along with dates seem to be infiltrating from outer space! Obviously more food stuffs coming on the railway instead of ammunition for front line.

American Air Force Arrives!

Flying Fortresses – bombing Pantelleria and Sicily ready for invasion of Italy. Quickly found our camp close by and becoming a big nuisance. Very generous with their better rations – all sorts of wonderful food in tins. However, there is a price to pay. They haunt our Mess and continually invite us to their camp. Their idea of relaxation between their bombing raids is two-day drunken parties. I attend one (famous band leaders and big band) but never again!

She said that the Americans had their own transport and always had a band with them. At the dances, the French girls had their chaperons - an aunt or grandmother, always dressed in black and keeping an eye on everything. They would vet the men first.

Mum and her colleagues did not have chaperons.

"The Americans were delighted because we didn't have a chaperon and so we were often whisked off onto the dance floor."

Day Duty

Little group of us have picnics by the railway line in the cool of the evening. Sunday afternoon tea parties. 'Hula' dances to gramophone records. One of our doctors on surgical side is a very keen dancer, whirled me off my feet several times! Much enjoyed the evening but I don't want to encourage him!

9th September

British and American forces land at Salerno. Tony was involved in this campaign.

Hospital fairly slack – we have a lot more free time. Dinner at RATD every Monday night, their rations better than ours. Lots of fun with friends but I am not all that keen with Tony heaven knows where! I do extra night duty. Worried about Tony. His unit part of the invasion of Italy.

October

Tony arrives in big convoy, sick and wounded from Italy – Salerno Landings. Visit frequently – progress slow but is winning. Not allowed up and I can't cart him off to the 'Hula Hula'. A party of us visit Constantine, Tony more or less convalescent but must take care <u>not to</u> <u>drink alcohol</u>. I don't think he did, but he certainly seems a bit high and someone dared him to climb the statue in the middle of the square opposite the Officers' Club. Huge female figure with enormous breasts – of course he <u>did</u> and sat on a breast – cheered on by the crowd now gathered!!
Tony pronounced fit and discharged to IRTD (Incident Response Training Department) *at Philippeville.*

Tony certainly enjoyed getting up to mischief and Mum would often tell us this particular story. On this occasion they had just had dinner at the Officers' Club and seeing the enormous statue was just too much for the men. Somebody turned to Tony and said, "I bet you wouldn't climb up there!" That's all they had to say and he was away.

The crowd gathered and then some soldiers turned up and Mum and her friend decided it was time to chicken out and make themselves scarce because they felt sure there was going to be trouble. Fortunately Tony did not get caught and wasn't arrested.

A change of staff occurs at the hospital.

*Miss Blore, our Matron, sent home, unfit for duty –
she hasn't been well all the time we've been here, too
old for Active Service.*

Awaiting replacement, another TAN (Territorial
Army Nurse) *I expect. Unfortunately they are too
'old school' for this sort of job.*

28th October

*Begin closing down the hospital – great excitement.
Where next?! Weather getting bad, COLD and some
rain.*

*Before saying farewell to the desert, the tents and the
everlasting SAND, flies, lizards – camping is out for
me forever – here are some amusing incidents I have
not so far recorded.*

*One blistering hot day about noon, standing with
Staff Skinner and Bailly outside my office tent, we
were amazed to see a startling sight. Suddenly there
appeared a large caravan of camels and sundry dark-
clothed Arabs moving slowly and with definite
purpose straight through the middle of our camp
from one end to the other. Not a word was said, not a
sound was made that we heard. Don't know whether
they were accosted by the Sgt. Major at the other
end, think not. They were a formidable sight.
Appears we had inadvertently pitched our tents on
an ancient track used over hundreds of years across*

the desert, and no way would they change their route for a few tents!

Another incident we thought very funny at the time but our Seniors did not, was soon after we arrived on the plain. Major Huff Wuff complained of thieving from his stores – tins of course, but also spare mosquito nets. He was inclined to think some of the orderlies were flogging them in Constantine rumoured to fetch £5 a net. Arab ladies were making them into dresses due to the nets being made of silk. One of our Officers claimed to have seen some garments in a shop in Constantine looking suspiciously as if made from mosquito nets!!

As for the food going missing, Huff Wuff at a bit of a loss but concluded Arabs were getting in at night unseen and unheard by the sentries! So he came up with a brilliant idea – single wire around stores, knee height, attach numerous empty tin cans. The noise was horrendous in the middle of the night.

1st November

Leave to Constantine with Tony, seven days. If he gets leave, I am also given leave automatically, with my Colonel's good wishes. I am to meet Tony in Constantine. An ambulance going that way so I get a lift. A truck overturns on the way there, just in front of our ambulance, Officer killed, and two others injured. Take them back to 31st General.

*Arrive at the Casino in Constantine two hours late –
Tony getting desperate! We had a little room at top
of Transit Hotel which was once the Grand Hotel,
now taken over by army. Very happy week. We had
lots of fun, and explored the ancient and marvellous
town. Dinner every night at the Casino, listening to
the orchestra and watching people – remember the
blond violinist, and the funny little man who played
the cello. Flashily dressed Arabs - obviously very rich
– some French Officers in splendid uniforms. What
unit? Must be attached to the Arabs! They looked as
if they had escaped from an Edwardian Musical
Comedy!*

*Tony had a cold, which I caught of course and
dampened our last two days. However, it was all
absolutely marvellous – so much in love with each
other- it's heaven.*

8th November Back to Chateaudun

*Feeling rather miserable. Reported back to Miss
Simpson, our new Matron, TAN and fortyish. She
arrived last week. Of course, she didn't know me, and
seemed very surprised that I had been on leave. Not
only surprised, but outraged! I had a distinct feeling
of unfriendliness here, obviously hadn't been told of
my absence. Explained the situation, husband on
leave so I got leave. She certainly didn't approve of
such 'goings on'. Of course, in her day, nurses didn't
marry. If they did, they left!! Not a good beginning.*

After spending time together and now having to be apart again, Tony is haunted by memories.

Tony's Letter

I'm writing this in our funny little room on the top floor. As I knew it would be, this place is haunted by you. Your perfume fills the place and there's a little mark here on the tablecloth made by your lipstick. On the floor there's a piece of gauze with which you dabbed at your pretty little nose.

The 103 Hospital begins to prepare to move on.

Bitterly cold nights, and daytime getting cold too. No patients now, nothing to do. A series of farewell dinners with our RATD friends and we still have our makeshift dance floor. Great news, Mary has become engaged to Peter, our dentist. His persistence has paid off. He got promptly posted to a Base Hospital, can't have lovers together in the same unit!

Packing up continues. There's nothing for us to do, all work done by our orderlies.
Two huge store tents close to our lines, full of camp beds and blankets. Two orderlies sleep in each tent supposedly looking after contents. We woke this morning to find the tents and contents had disappeared but the orderlies were sleeping peacefully where the tents had been! Hadn't heard a thing. The Major, our Quarter Master, hopping mad!

Got news, Tony back in hospital 100th Base Hospital Philippeville, abscess on bottom!

While Tony is in hospital he longs for a glimpse of Joy and expects to see her again any day.

100th Base Hospital

I understand that you should have arrived here last Friday but that it was postponed, as these things usually are. Matron is due to arrive this evening so you can't be very far behind. I'm getting terribly excited – every time I hear female footsteps I can't help expecting to see you walk into the ward. It's really only a few days since I was last with you but it seems like an age, and already I'm starving for a glimpse of your sweet face again.

What is wonderful about reading the diary and reading the letters is that amongst the serious drama and emotional ups-and-downs are little delightfully amusing stories. The next one is such an example. Back to Tony's letters again.

12th November The Sociable Chicken

The Mess here owns two hundred chickens of assorted varieties which supply us with the odd egg at breakfast-time and an occasional 'game dish' on special occasions. One of these fowls is called Patricia and during the last week she has taken up residence in the ante-room. Every evening she appears at about half-past five and establishes herself comfortably on the back of the best chair in the Mess. And there she stays, presumably until the mess staff clean the place out in the morning. If she's disturbed she just clucks round until she finds another comfortable chair and perches there. Queer thing is that she's not happy until she's right in the middle of everybody which of course is in the vicinity of the bar.

The 103 Hospital is now on the move and the diary describes the difficult journey.

26th November We move to Philippeville

Horrid, bumpy, long, cold journey, though got much warmer as we came off the plain, and reached the sea. Several of us go to the 100th in transit, what luck.

Tony allowed up, and can leave the hospital but must be back on his ward by nightfall! And of course, I have to be in a different part!   However, we have some glorious days by the sea – very happy again. Go to the Officers' Club for dinner and dancing every night. Go shopping and buy a lot of dates, melons and oranges. We have our favourite, special place on the sand to eat them, and have taken to reading aloud to each other.

They take time to pose for a studio photograph and amongst Tony's letters is this revealing comment.

11th December The Photograph

I can't say it's particularly good. You look positively startled and I've got the most absurdly fatuous grin all over my pan, and together we look rather like an advertisement for a new brand of toothpaste. But the fact remains that it is a photograph of us together, and that fact alone makes it my most treasured possession.

Mum is in a reflective mood as she thinks about all that has happened.

12th December Reflections

We sat in our usual place today and talked a little about the future. Now I'm back in our temporary quarters, sort of dormitory, Tony gone back to his ward.

At Another Crossroads.

Looking back on these extraordinary and eventful months, can hardly believe so much has happened so quickly. Last Autumn began our whirlwind romance. Joined the QAs, posting to Leeds Castle, Christmas... No way did I think I would be married before the next one! Posting to severely bombed Southampton Netley Hospital – no patients but a centre for mobilization for overseas. All the time, almost daily letters, wonderful letters from Tony always declaring his love for me - then they stopped for a while. This meant only one thing – he must have left the country - where? But I soon know, our 'code' worked! And at last I had an address for him – North Africa – 1st Army.

That cold February at Netley, miserable place, and uncertain of the future. Tony's love letters were a great solace. I have them all. Don't laugh at me as I know you will when you read this. You wanted me to keep a diary. It isn't exactly that, but I have recorded what thoughts might amuse one day.

My arrival in Algiers to find you wounded and in a Base Hospital with a broken leg in plaster and other nasty wounds, recovery likely to be a long job, you deemed it to be a bonus, the fates decreeing we should cement our love for each other and marry forthwith. We are so young yet the war has made us so much older than our years.

And so to the desert and our Field Hospital; some ghastly days, some funny days, some only just bearable days! But thank goodness for a sense of humour and some very good friends.

And so we get married. Tony back to his unit, training for the next move the war will take. We have the odd leave together, blissfully happy. Who knows what tomorrow will bring? With it all you remain optimistic, so sure we have a happy future ahead in a calmer world.

Now another parting looms tomorrow as the next day I shall be gone to Italy, leaving you to finish your convalescence and then back to your unit somewhere in Italy too. Light awfully bad in this place, better find my bed.

13th December We sail for Italy

HMS Dorsetshire, rather old and shabby, whole unit on board. As the sun sets we leave the harbour, my friend Mary and I standing together by the rail watching the lights on the coast grow dim, thinking of Peter and Tony sadly watching us go. Rough crossing, lots of people sick – fortunately I'm a good sailor.

Tony is not supposed to know where or when she went but he has a rough idea and goes down to the harbour hoping to catch just a glimpse of her ship. He stays and watches.

Tony's Letter

My dear,
I walked all the morning and in the afternoon I bought some tangerines and went down to 'our spot'. It was a foolish thing to do really. I tried to read, but all the time I was watching the harbour entrance. Went to tea at

four o'clock and when I reappeared at about five, there you were about four miles away. At least I presume it was you.

There's not much I can say to you, my sweet. Your sad sweet face as you waited for the ambulance haunts me. If you hadn't wept a little, it is more than likely that I would have done – and that would never do. But with the prospect of seeing you again soon, the future looks quite bright.

So until we meet again, be cheerful, my dearest heart. God bless you and keep you safe.

From your adoring Tony

Tony and Joy, Algiers

Washing very primitive,
Canvas basin for everything
body or clothes.

Joy 1943

Italy

Mum arrives in Italy where war has left its devastating mark.

16th December Naples

7am sailing into the breathtaking beauty of the Bay of Naples, calm sea now and the sun shining brightly but then as we get closer, we notice that the harbour is littered with damaged ships, the buildings behind in ruins. Impossible for ship to dock properly, gets as close as possible. Ropes are fixed across and we had to clamber over upturned ships' bottoms (!) clinging to the ropes – very slippery, very scary! Helped up onto the dockside, man-handled really! However, we got there and found several ambulances waiting to transport us further. Drove away through crowds of people shouting and throwing flowers at us. What a welcome!

Hectic drive through battle-scarred streets, damaged buildings all around. Long bumpy drive out into rural countryside. Arrive at Castellamare – Transit camp. Huge impressive building. We are told that it was once a famous palace – could have fooled me! Later it became a renowned hotel. During German occupation used as hospital for wounded. Building now badly damaged.

Situated half way up a mountainside and proved to be overrun by RATS, fleas and bugs of all description. Drainage and water system nil and you wouldn't believe the PONG!! This apparently was the best on offer as a temporary lodging while our men folk set off to scan the countryside for a suitable place to be our hospital. They tell us it has to be in a special area with access to something that is about to occur!

The stove

We were given a very large smelly room on the top floor, bleak and bare, with broken shutters at the windows. The only items of furniture are four iron beds with very suspect mattresses. In the middle of the room is a large, iron, wood-burning stove, chimney going up through the ceiling, NOT alright and very dirty. Our bed rolls arrived – very damp. Unfortunately getting luggage off the ship had understandably been somewhat difficult and a few things got dropped in the water – had certainly touched it!! We looked around in dismay. It was bitterly cold – something must be done about that STOVE.

"Let's explore," I suggested.
We found plenty of trees and woody undergrowth in what must once have been the grounds. We gathered as much kindling and logs and bits that we could carry back to our garret. Mair, the practical one,

always carries a goodly amount of toilet rolls, essential luggage, now to prove their worth in another way. While others watched in trepidation, I stuffed a quantity of toilet roll paper into the stove, followed by kindling and matches. Hey Presto! We had warmth. Very popular with all our other friends. "Please show us how to do it," they said.

No bathrooms, no running water, had to collect one pint each in biscuit tins from downstairs, had to do for everything. Had our cook with us and a couple of orderlies. Food very basic, mainly bully beef. We were often reduced to drinking hot water with marmite mixed in.

Although bitterly cold and snow higher up the mountains, we had marvellous walks through the forest, scrambling along goat tracks. Gather firewood – rule of the house, never go walking without coming back with a bundle of wood!
Not long before the word got out and we were visited (and indeed rescued) by RA Officers from nearby Battery. Better food and added bonus, TRANSPORT! Got to Naples or what's left of it, very badly bombed.

Army taken over one fairly decent building, must have been a 'posh' hotel, now a pretty good Officers' Club. Our new friends managed to organise a couple of rather hectic parties.

Back in North Africa, Tony goes into Philippeville and joins a group of people. He gets a lift in a truck full of Officers going to the Casino.

19th December

It's remarkable how pally men can become under these circumstances. I'd never seen this crowd before in my life but by ten o'clock we were all slapping each other on the back and telling each other what jolly good types we were. As usual, there were a lot of very rowdy Canadians and Americans there; in fact the situation became so tense that the Field Officer of the day ordered that no more drinks were to be served after 10.30, much to everybody's annoyance.

The result of all this is that you didn't have a letter written to you yesterday and I've had a head like an iron-foundry all day today.

20th December

Hope you had a good journey. I was terribly worried at the time, but as we've had no news I suppose everything is alright.

21st December

I've spent quite a busy day today helping to decorate the ward for Christmas. We're all very enthusiastic about it and it's very amusing and great fun. We've put little dots of cotton wool all over the windows to represent snow. The lights are shaded with army form blank and the ceiling and walls are festooned with bandages, dyed with gentian violet, brilliant green and aquamarine. And of course the whole place is littered with the nearest approach to holly we can find. As yet we haven't found a substitute for mistletoe, but no doubt some bright spark will think of something.

This evening I've been down to the club and used my influence to order some drink for the ward. They were very co-operative and tomorrow they're going to deliver enough drink to float a battleship – forty bottles of mixed booze. There's only fourteen of us to deal with it so we should have quite a party.

I'm now sitting in the ante-room writing this on a magazine covered with your handwriting – the scores of that game of dominoes you taught me.

Meanwhile in Italy, they also get ready for their Christmas celebrations.

Christmas Eve

All rather homesick. Decorate our room, drew funny pictures on the walls. Collected evergreens and stuff that looked like holly. Got invited and escorted to dance at Officers' Con. Home in Sorrento.

Christmas Day

In better spirits. After lunch at RA Mess served 'tea' to the lads on lovely green site amid cheers and shouts of joy. Back in the Mess for dinner, everything laid on. Where did they get it?? Dance and concert afterwards.

Boxing Day

Big post in today, stacks of letters from Tony. Dinner again with RA friends. Another party, another dance!

30th December

Super dance at the Officers' Con. Home at Sorrento, had a marvellous time – feeling a bit guilty knowing Tony working hard – retraining and getting ready to rejoin his unit. I seem to be having all the fun, but it can't last.

Tony's Christmas celebrations have finally come to an end.

I think we really have finished the Christmas season at last. We kept it up as long as we could, but by midday today even the most ardent spirits were beginning to flag. Champagne at breakfast-time is all very nice once or twice but the strain begins to tell after a time.

We really have had quite a good time and frankly I've enjoyed it. It's the same old story though – if only you had been here. If you had, things would have been very different.

Every day by two o'clock, the place looked more like a bar parlour rather than an Officers' ward in a military hospital. But I don't think you can blame us. For the majority of these boys there's not much consolation to be found otherwise and bags of no future.

He has been making his daily pilgrimage down to the beach and writes,

Our spot on the beach is very much the same. I've convinced myself that the impression of your body is still on the sand.

At long last he suddenly gets a burst of news.

31st December

It's happened! It's happened! It's happened! Nine letters all from you arrived last night and I haven't got over it yet. When I got over the first excitement I was furious 'cos they'd been held up. Do you know those bloody fools at IRTD, instead of sending them straight down here by ambulance or something, they'd waited 'til about fifteen arrived then sent them back to the APO (Army Post Office)*to be re-sorted and re-delivered. Phooey!*

But dearest heart, what wonderful letters. I'm on top of the world again now. I was prepared for the first few letters to be a bit sad but how glad I am that the last few seemed to be fairly cheerful. The last letter was written on 23rd December so that's not too bad really.

Your episode in the back street with the soldiers (that sounds awful doesn't it?) must have been most alarming. Do take care my sweet. Remember you're all I have, and if anything should happen to you I should go quite mad. Nevertheless, I'm absurdly proud of you.

Good night my sweet. It won't be long before we can be together again. Just wait for me to come to you again and then I'll make you forget that you've ever been unhappy while we've been apart.

You have all of me. From Tony.

There is no mention of the incident with the soldiers in the diary but it does give us some insight into how dangerous or alarming life could be.

Mum and the other Sisters are now on the move again.

New Year's Eve

What a day, rained buckets and we move to Nocera to open our hospital.

Nocera

Dreadful buildings – leaking roof, what's left of them, half the windows missing, broken shutters, no lights, no heating and no water in the taps. Local population had sheltered in it during fighting and left all their mess behind. Retreating Germans had blown up mains and sewer. We surveyed it all in horror. Told it must be ready to receive patients in two weeks!

Tony knows the place well. He writes,

If you are where I think you are, then you're plumb in the middle of the scene of the most ghastly battle I've ever had the misfortune to experience. Is the hospital nearly at the top of a hill, looking up the valley? But don't let that worry you my sweet – I shall be terribly interested to see it all again at my leisure this time.

He continues to comment in another letter.

Isn't it amazing that you should go to, well- where you have gone to. I think I said something about it in a previous letter. We knew that place as Hospital Hill, and by God how we knew it. Honestly Joy, we actually had a battle in the hospital. One of my sections actually shot at Huns on the roof. I'm longing to get back there to have a look at it again. And that's not the only reason.

Much later Tony receives more information about the conditions and makes this next remark.

Had some letters from home – most of them sympathising with you about your troubles when you first arrived at your new hospital. Of course that shook me no end, because having had none of your earlier letters, I'd no idea that things had been so grim.

My poor sweet, was it very awful? Hope to God things are better by now.

An awful thing has happened. Got up rather late this morning and went to Algiers but I didn't have time to shave. Went to a barber's shop and amongst other things had my moustache trimmed. I've always been a bit worried about it – it's been getting a bit out of hand just lately. However, when I was having a wash at the club about an hour later, I realized that the silly old bugger (excuse me) had pruned it down until it looked as though it had been drawn with an eye-brow pencil. I looked like a bloody spiv! So I dashed out into the nearest barber's shop and had the whole damn lot taken off. Hope you approve. I was simply livid!

1944

The 103rd Hospital is busy preparing the abandoned building into a working hospital.

New Year's Day

We begin work! Orderlies marvellous. RE did wonders to restore basic lighting and plumbing. We swept out the muck and disinfected everything! Very busy throughout January, convoys of wounded plus, plus. Some really bad cases.

Working on B2 surgical and have my faithful Bailly back, now Nursing Orderly 1st class, always by my side. We work long hours but better to have something to do again.

Tony sent back to Algiers, but think it's only temporary.

1st January The 100th General Hospital Algiers

For the last thirty six hours there's been the most extraordinary gale blowing. A terribly strong wind played havoc with the tents and most of us were up until about one o'clock moving the helpless patients into huts. We put them all over the place, in the showers, in the massage hut, the operating theatre and even in the dining rooms. This morning the place was a complete shambles. Not one of the Sisters' tents was left standing and lots of the girls have lost everything, either blown away or buried under about three feet of wet sand. One wretched girl spent the night on a shelf in the linen room on our ward. Nobody knew about it – but imagine the comments when we were told this morning.

It's simply poured with rain and on several occasions there have been hail storms with lumps of hail as big as peas. Went into P'ville this afternoon and the sea was breaking onto the road. I can't remember ever having experienced anything quite like it before. It's gradually dying down, but the wind is still blowing a gale and there are sudden torrential downpours of rain.

What a year 1943 was. Certainly the most eventful in my short life. In those twelve months, I've known every emotion possible for a human being, from the depths of despair to the heights of sheer, perfect happiness.

Tony goes on to say that when he was low, it was Joy who had pulled him through.

He keeps quite busy over the next few days.

3rd January

The weather has cleared up at last – thank God. From what I read in the Union Jack you had the same show in your part of the world. Pretty bloody awful wasn't it? Tonight though it's very lovely here. There's a grand moon and just enough white clouds to make it beautiful. How I wish that you were here to enjoy it with me and to walk along the beach, hand-in-hand.

My existence here is becoming even more idle. Yesterday I went down to the beach just to make sure that there was nothing left of our spot and there wasn't. It made me rather sad to think that something which we had shared had vanished. So today I haven't moved further than the Mess. But there's now an overflow of patients into the hut where you were sleeping, and so for twenty minutes, I made polite conversation to somebody I'd never seen before in my life just for the sake of being somewhere where you had been.

Apart from that, I've read, played cards and dominoes and talked. Lord, how we talk. We talk about anything and everything. When there are a lot of us it's generally an exchange of war experiences and when there's just two of us it's generally about the people we love.

6th January

We've had two film shows in succession yesterday and today. Yesterday it was George Formby (can't stand that man) but tonight it was 'Five Graves to Cavio' and a damn good film it was too. When it was over we came back to a grand curry dinner. Very welcome 'cos it's bitterly cold here nowadays. After dinner I read your letters again.

Sorry to hear your nighties have shocked the nuns, poor things. You are keeping the white one for me aren't you, my sweet?

Then I boiled myself in a steaming hot bath and now I'm sitting in bed feeling all pink and warm and clean, smoking, sipping at a cup of tea and writing to you. So on the whole life is not too bad, but oh how I miss you!

Tony considers joining the SAS (Special Air Service) Regiment to get out of infantry battalions, but only gets as far as making enquires.

He tries desperately to re-join his unit so that he can get to Italy.

10th January

I was discharged from the 100th with a recommendation for seven days sick leave. I thought I could be posted straight to the IRTD when they reached their destination, so I went to the Transit Camp to wait for them. However, the Commandant told me quite calmly that I would be going down to Algiers in a few days. You see the IRTD have stopped receiving anybody ex-hospital for the time being.

Anyway I nearly threw a fit and rushed up to IRTD to see Colonel Stott. Incidentally, by the time I arrived, No 4 Battalion was already on board. Old man Stott received me with open arms. He said that of course I could go to them – he'd have a word with a pal of his.

However, it did not work out and he remains in North Africa for a bit longer. He does mention that he keeps everything packed ready for a sudden move.

17th January   A Brawl in Algiers

Got mixed in up in an awful brawl at the Casino last night. A drunken American in the Merchant Navy ran amok with a knife. He stabbed a Gendarme and all hell was let loose. Chairs, tables, bottles and glasses flying all over the place just like a wild western film. When there were no more glasses left for me to throw – merely in self-defence I assure you – I grabbed hold of a WAAC who was getting rather worried about things and sat her on the ground in a corner and bent over her – things were really getting a bit desperate. All I got for my troubles was a chair in the back of the neck.

Eventually the bloke who had caused all the trouble made a dash for the stairs and went. We all breathed a sigh of relief, finished our drinks, and left. At the bottom of the stairs was the trouble maker, lying on the floor handcuffed and bleeding from about twelve different wounds. The Gendarmes had got him and taken his knife away. We made sure that an ambulance was on the way and then went – toute de suite. So you see I've had quite a busy time just lately.

21st January   A Court- Marshal

On Tuesday a French concert party visited the camp. It was the best show I've seen anywhere, in England or Africa. I laughed so much I hurt myself and frankly I enjoyed it much better than the Leslie Henson show. There were some very fetching girls too, lots of 'em, which pleased the lads no end. In fact one of them would have fetched anything from a millionaire to a fox terrier.

In the middle of the show I got a message telling me that I was to sit on a court-marshal in Algiers at nine o'clock next morning. I'd never done anything like that before, so I sat up until one o'clock reading the Manual of Military Law and the Rules of Procedure for Court Marshals.

The affair went off quite well. The wretched man was terribly worked up about it all and thank God we found him not guilty. It was all very amusing in parts because the witnesses included a Frenchwoman, an Arab woman and some Italian prisoners. There were two interpreters, English – French and French – Italian. When the Italians appeared, we spoke to the Englishman who told the Frenchman who told the Italian and then all the way back. I nearly went grey. One Italian was so stupid; he didn't seem to understand a thing. Nobody could stop him talking and he succeeded in getting everybody so muddled that the prosecuting Officer gave up in despair and said he'd do without him. The Arab woman created a diversion by bringing her small baby into the court with her. The most engaging little creature, who cooed, gurgled and spluttered the whole time and quite upset the gravity of the occasion.

We'd finished by twelve thirty and I had lunch at the club. Met a lot of friends with the inevitable results. Why is it that men always have to drink when they get together? I'm sure it's because of the life we have to lead. Met a sailor too, with a plaster on his leg like mine. He'd just been thrown out of the convalescent depot at Chenoua for being drunk for three days. A thoroughly good type, you'll understand. We spent the evening together. We varied the usual routine by doing a Café crawl from one end of the Rue Michelet to the other. We eventually ended up at two this morning in the new bar I told you about. I slept on his ship, a fleet tender. This morning I was down by a pair of new gloves and several hundred francs.

Got back here in time for lunch. Nobody had missed me – this really is an amazing place.

28th January

My dear one,
Had my first letter from you for nearly four weeks today. Most important news- Bing Crosby and Bob Hope are coming very soon. Hope to see Nancy very soon.

30th January   Orderly Officer

I've been Orderly Officer today and what a bloody awful job that is too. I've mounted five different guards this afternoon at five different hives and duly inspected them all at their posts. When I've finished this letter I've got to go round the whole damn lot again, and in the pitch black night and it's extremely cold. Thank God I've got a good Orderly Sergeant on with me.

Part of my duties are to inspect the compound where the prisoners serving sentences are kept. There're about one hundred and fifty of them and it's just like a zoo. Never have I met such an awful collection of individuals. Most of them are in for desertion and boy are they mutinous as all they want is to be kept in there for as long as possible to avoid any fighting. Most of them have got five or six years anyway.

Mum has voiced concerns about the attitude of her superiors in a letter to Tony. There is no mention of this in the diary. She also seems to have written about seeing some of the horrors of war as the wounded are brought in.

In his next letter Tony responds to her concerns.

31st January

My darling,

Please don't let your worries get you down. Don't let the condition of those poor lads depress you – remember that they probably think they're the lucky ones. And as for the attitude of your superiors – well that shouldn't upset you so very much. You should know, after a year in the army that one doesn't have to pay much attention to that kind of thing. You know that you're doing a damn fine job. And if you don't, well I do, and so do countless other people.

God knows, but I realise only too well how easily one can get depressed under these circumstances. More often than I like to remember, I feel myself slipping into the bluest of blue moods. But, if you think of it, neither of us have any right to feel miserable. We've had the most amazing good fortune so far. Things aren't so bad really, you know. This state of affairs can't last for very much longer. Just a few more months and then we shan't have to write letters like this.

Meanwhile, the hospital at Nocera continues to function fairly smoothly.

Things settle down. Our Mess quite decent now cleaned up. Food has improved slightly, plenty of fruit and wonders of wonders, cauliflowers galore!

Mum told me there had been the most marvellous cauliflowers, huge ones, all growing in the fields. They had not seen green vegetables for months and months.

Getting some off-duty time now, the odd party and dinners at the Officers' Club in Naples. When having lunch at Officers' Club in Naples with Frances, crowded dining room, was asked by head waiter, could two other Officers share our table? Of course! It was a Colonel Prodgers and his Adjutant! We were somewhat taken back. However, they proved very pleasant and chatty, rather friendly in fact. Col. offered to drive us back to Nocera in his staff car – arrived back in state – a few raised eyebrows!

Mid January

Hospital busy but getting regular off-duty time. Col. Prodgers in touch – I seem to have made a hit in high quarters!

Took me to Amalfi, very beautiful marvellous drive around the coast, sensational views, staff car and driver. A few days later, Col Prodgers sent message inviting me to accompany him to a dance in Salerno. When we got there, I was very surprised to find we were the guests of honour!
And worse – embarrassed to find Matron there – way down the table!
Oh dear!

4th February Night Duty

Leaving the Mess I am not surprised to find Bailly waiting outside to carry my bag. He always manages to make the change with me. I don't ask but I am very grateful that he chooses to work with me.

As we walk across the square to our Ward Block, Vesuvius looms large and menacing, large flames and sparks reaching into the sky. Bailly casts a wary eye and gruffly announces, "That's going to blow up one of these days Sister!"
I laughed and said, "No! It's safe enough, been like that for hundreds of years."

Happy, happy reunion, two days together. Tony has acquired a flat in village. We discuss our future plans in some depth. Tony has decided he wants to stay in the army. They are already seeking out the young men who will form the basis of the Regular Peacetime Army and he wants to be part of this. He sees our future based on what he is learning and training for now. Tony goes back to Naples for War Office Board and passes out in highest grade for a Regular Commission.

Tony goes to IRTD north of Naples – very, very busy.

Tony seems to be excited that he is now an instructor on a course. He writes in more detail.

27th February

Joy my dearest heart,
So much has happened just lately that I literally have not had the time to or the opportunity to write.

The course on which I am instructing started properly on Thursday. I'm thoroughly enjoying it - it's quite a pleasant change to do some work for once, and what is more, to feel that you really are doing something worthwhile. I get on well with the chaps. I find that it's far easier to instruct Officers than private soldiers. The group of which I am in charge is called 'C' syndicate. They've christened me 'The King of C'. We have to work hard too. All day we are either lecturing or supervising and in the evening we have the next day's work to prepare. I'm generally pretty tired by dinner time, and after that, having swatted up my notes for the next day, it's all I can do to clamber into bed.

On the Thursday I was turned out of my billet because Battalion Headquarters was moving in. I made desperate efforts to find another room for myself – but failed. Managed to stay under a roof for Thursday night but on Friday I had to move into a tent. At about eleven o'clock at night it started to rain and later, it started to blow and hard too. By three o'clock in the morning, I decided to evacuate. So, clad in boots and pyjamas only, I moved into the store tent. On the way I stumbled into a ditch with two feet of water in it! Myself and my blankets were consequently soaked with water. I salvaged what I could of my kit (your photo in my map case was the first article), but I had to leave the rest. Having battened down my tent, I put my trust in God, and went to bed again.

I got up at seven o'clock to find my tent about fifty yards away from where I had last seen it. I literally hadn't got a stitch of dry clothing or equipment to wear. So I went to the CQMS's store and got dressed straight off his shelves. I was in a flat spin, and to make things worse my batman had gone on a draft the day before. However, in between lectures I managed to find myself a room. At the present I am busily engaged in trying to dry my stuff over a charcoal brazier. It's quite a nice room too, and I haven't found any lice – yet!

So you see I've had a pretty hectic time. Still no letter from you. I can't think what's happening to them. Please God that one comes soon.

I must go to bed now my sweet. I can hardly keep my eyes open. God keep you safe for me.
From your devoted Tony.

In the diary Mum considers all the things that are happening. There is a feeling of change and excitement in the air.

Time for Reflection

Those few days we had before Tony left and we talked about our future and how the war was going, victories in Italy as the allies force their way up the centre of Italy. Tony knows his unit is up to something special – not telling me exactly of course.

Things hotting up at home – hundreds of American Troops massing in England, obviously getting ready for an invasion of France. Letters from home full of it, and not all complementary to the USA! One or two of my patients express concern, wives telling of rowdy parties, nylons as gifts, how the Yanks have money to burn! I try to ease their worries, since their wives wouldn't write about it if they had anything to hide!

Mum said that they were very pleased to have the Americans with them, as they brought a lot of manpower and much needed equipment.

I digress. We feel strongly and hopeful that the war will soon be over. Tony very optimistic and he also thinks he will soon be upgraded to Captain – more money – we do so want to start a family – shall we go for it? The time seems right.

They both felt that the war was not going to last much longer and in her words, "We felt we were both getting on a bit. That's when couples did start their families. We didn't want to waste any more time."

There was an incident in Italy during the war that Mum used to tell us about which involved one of her staff and reflects the harsh conditions at the time.

Tumi's Story

Tumi was one of Mum's orderlies, a GDO. He was a lovely cockney lad but a bit simple, a nice guy though. One day he came to Mum and asked if he could have some extra tins of corn beef.

"Why, what are you going to do with that?" she asked.

Tumi explained that he and a friend had gone into the local village and a man had approached them and said that if they would give him some corned beef, he would let them sleep with one of his daughters.

"Tumi, you shouldn't do that!" said Mum.

She had a word with Staff Sergeant Skinner, told him what had happened and suggested, "I think you'd better have a quiet word with Tumi and give him some fatherly advice."

The Italians were starving. Sicily and Naples had been badly bombed. They were short of food, and the British Army's food supplies were also very low.

In Mum's own words, "You can't really imagine what it was like unless you've actually experienced it. These days it's hard to believe that it was like that, but it was."

Night duty progresses fairly quietly. These very fit, tough, mostly young men recover from their wounds quickly and especially as we have this magic new drug, penicillin. Have been told we are the first hospital to try it out.

Mum said the results were miraculous. They had never seen anything like it before. Wounds that used to take a long time to heal, now suddenly healed very rapidly.

It just so happens that I know the daughter of the boy who was one of the first civilians to be treated with penicillin in Britain. What follows is his account.

John's Story

In 1943, John Hayter was 10 years old. While playing 'tip it and run' at Hanworth School, Middlesex, the air raid siren went off. This could happen quite often because the Germans were targeting the airfield near the school. The air raid shelters were situated on the playing fields and the children and teachers would just have time to grab their gas mask cases and sandwiches and rush down to sit on the benches that lined the shelters.

It was always cold in there. On this particular occasion, during the hectic few minutes of trying to get forty young children to the safety of the air raid shelters, there was a lot of pushing and shoving and John was kicked on his left foot. There was no time to clean the wound properly at the time and no more thought was given to it. However, a few weeks later, John was experiencing serious pain and inflammation in his injured foot. He was taken to visit his doctor, whose response was that John was suffering from 'growing pains'.

Within a few days John's whole leg was inflamed and he was admitted to Ward D2, The Children's Ward of Staines Emergency County Hospital, London. It had been set up to deal with the overflow of casualties from the London bombings. On arrival at the hospital John's consultant, Mr. Woodwalker, was unsure of a diagnosis. It was another doctor, who on sight of John's x-ray, diagnosed Osteomyelitis, (a severe infection of the bone). He had seen many cases of this whilst he had been treating soldiers from the trenches during World War One.

Given the diagnosis, John's parents were then presented with the choice of either having John's leg amputated, or allowing an operation to be performed in which an attempt would be made to drill away the contaminated bone and infection. They opted for the operation.

John subsequently spent the next nine months recovering from the operation with his leg in plaster from the knee down. During this time he had two companions, Arthur Lovett and Ronnie Currington, two other children who were long-term patients in the beds adjacent to his. Arthur had an illness relating to his lungs and unfortunately died. John and Ronnie were never told that he had died, he just disappeared one day and the matter was not discussed. Ronnie had been burnt from his neck to his heels and spent all his recovery time on his stomach.

Although this was a Children's Ward, the parents were only allowed to 'view' their children at 2.30 pm on a Wednesday or Sunday afternoon through slits in the ward doors. Face-to-face contact was prohibited as it was believed that this would 'unsettle' the children. However, John would receive a tin from his parents every day. In the tin would be some kind of treat, wafer biscuits and sweets - just little things that were a welcome change from the normal hospital food.

The Children's Ward backed on to the Admissions Area of the hospital and was also used as an overflow ward for those who had been admitted with terrible injuries from the bombings. John and his companions frequently witnessed the injured being brought into hospital on stretchers before and after being treated by the doctors.

At one point John's consultant thought that, just like patients recovering from tuberculosis, John should be kept in his bed outside, all day and all night, only coming back on to the ward for bed baths and treatment. This continued for several months. His bed would be pushed outside onto a hard standing area. There was a metal cradle over his foot and a rubber sheet was placed over the bedcoverings. At night, the nurses would put their cloaks on and come out and check on their young patient.

"Are you alright John?" they would enquire and see if he needed a hot-water bottle.

It was at night that the skyline would come alive, lit up with the bomb explosions and subsequent fires burning from the Blitz.

After his discharge from hospital John suffered many 'flare-ups' of the infection and was constantly readmitted. At this time the American doctors that were based there were trying out an experimental drug called Penicillin. They had been using it on American troops suffering from venereal disease. Although the drug was readily available, the hospital only had very limited access to it. Eventually, it was decided that it should be used in John's treatment. The drug was administered via syringe in the buttocks eight times in a twenty-four-hour period over several weeks. The drug was recycled from John's urine, sent to the hospital laboratory to be refined, and then re-injected into him.

The result was that the infection was abated and John survived, one of the first civilians to be given Penicillin.

Over the next 70 years John has suffered several flare ups of the disease, the last time was during the 1990s. He is still prescribed Penicillin. Ironically, his daughter is allergic to the drug.

Now, back to the diary.

9th March

Bailly somehow gets me very pleasant meals (middle of the night). This friend of his in the Cook House must have secret resources! The other Sisters are complaining about the standard of the meals – I don't comment!

Begin my nights off. Horrid disappointment, Tony doesn't think he will be able to get away.

10th March

Very miserable all day – just about rock bottom when he is announced at 7pm! We depart to our flat in village. Enough said!

11th March

We visit Pompei and the famous ruins.

Start off with a guide and a bag of apples. We have the place to ourselves – not another soul. Our guide doesn't speak much English and Tony's Italian lends more to the theatre than actual spoken word! Our progress is hilarious. Spent two hours, fantastic place, much of it so beautiful. Also building of 'delights'. I wasn't allowed to see some of these. The guide insisted I stayed outside a certain building, not for innocent female eyes. Tony allowed in, so I made him tell me what I had missed! Hardly mind boggling, I'm not that innocent! What did impress us was that the 'Ancients' were a jolly sight cleaner than people of today!

Also visited the Cathedral, splendid and overpowering. Over-decorated, I thought, gave me a 'funny' feeling – too RC (Roman Catholic).

Salerno club for dinner, then got pulled into a party. Afraid I got a bit pickled. Returned home in very good spirits!

12th March Sunday

Quiet day, lunch in Salerno. Raining hard all day. On duty that night. Tony comes on with me.

13th March

Last twenty four hours together. In a few days Tony goes to Anzio.

14th March

Watch Tony drive off. Very sad, wonder when I shall see him again. Going on duty this evening feeling rather sad, however our weekend was rather fun, and there will be other leaves.

Looking up at Vesuvius it seems a bit livelier, bigger flames, more smoke and strange rumbles!? Bailly doesn't like the look of it but then he never does!

20th March Vesuvius Erupts!!!

7am, Bailly brought my tea. Time to start work. He opens the shutters – black outside. Should be light? Day staff come on, still not getting light. Above, heavy black pall and nasty smell of sulphur! Much speculation, must be Vesuvius, what else? In the Mess, told to, "Keep calm, behave as normal."

Night staff to our sleeping quarters, separate building from the Mess, other side of the square. Surprisingly, did go to sleep.

Awakened at 3pm by our batmen with orders from the Colonel to get up, pack a bag with essentials only, and get across to the Mess. The roof of our building in danger of collapse! Shocked to discover that the rather grand steps, twelve I think, leading up to the door, had disappeared under a grey smoking mass of ash and cinders! The level of the square had risen considerably higher, covered in ashes over which we had to walk. We could feel the heat through the soles of our shoes!

Ashes pouring down all day and getting deeper. Roofs collapsing, roads blocked, movement on them impossible.
We are completely marooned!

The story of Vesuvius had always fascinated me. With every retelling, she would add a little more detail or give an extra bit of insight. She made it sound so exciting, and enjoyed sharing it. Remember those marvellous cauliflowers that were mentioned earlier? Well, as Mum said, "We had all those wonderful cauliflowers and of course Vesuvius killed the lot. We did manage to eat some before that happened."

State of Emergency Announced.

However Colonel says we must cope somehow.
A very gloomy Bailly turned up at 8pm to escort me across to the ward. Give him his due, he didn't say, "I told you so!"

Nightmare Week.

We were cut off for two or three days. Much damage to our buildings. Pioneer Corp sent to dig us out and clear a route through to the port for our ambulances. Looking around, what a sight it is – crops ruined, everywhere half-buried. Some houses in the village had completely disappeared. Nearer the volcano, two villages buried under lava. Took a month for us to get back to normal working. On the second night, some soldiers turned up completely lost.

The Colonel called us all together for an emergency meeting – earthquake likely, following such an enormous eruption – or so the Italian authorities warned. First sign, movement of hanging-light fittings, get out of building immediately, not to try and get patients out –no time before collapse of buildings. If uninjured, we more useful after, helping in rescue work. Shocking, but saw the sense of it.
Told to tell orderlies the situation. Pray it won't happen.

Tony's Letter

I understand that old Vesuvius has been misbehaving itself. It certainly was a magnificent sight when I left Naples nearly a fortnight ago. And I hear too that Nocera has been literally smothered in ashes. Poor old Joy. You do pick some unpleasant spots to live in. I do hope that it hasn't been too unpleasant. The weather up here has been fairly good. Thank God, and I'm getting quite sunburnt again.

His next letter contrasts vividly with the experience that Mum is facing after the eruption of Vesuvius.

English Daisies

My dearest,
The weather is still grand – thank the Lord. This isn't a particularly beautiful bit of country but the spring flowers are beginning to show themselves and you're liable to suddenly stumble upon the most beautiful little corners. And to my surprise there are hundreds of common or garden English daisies. They seem quite out of place and the first time I saw them it made me feel very homesick. And there are the sweetest little violets. When I get the chance I'll gather some and send them to you in exchange for the ones I have that belong to you.

The hospital at Nocera has now returned to normal after the chaos caused by the eruption and runs smoothly again.

1st April day duty E1

Been a few staff changes. Met some new Sisters from England. They seemed a bit lost, not quite what they expected. They were used to huge wards, long rooms divided into six bays on each side, ten beds in each bay – one hundred and twenty – three Sisters each ward, twelve orderlies. We share an office and sort out the bays between us, roughly forty patients each. Told them they should be pleased they missed the desert if they think this is bad!

The battle of Anzio

The battle of Anzio lasted from the 22nd January to the 5th June. It is highly likely that Tony was involved in a lot of this but, of course, he can not specify this in his letters.

The diary mentions that a lot of wounded were coming from this area.

Since going to Anzio I've had lots of letters from Tony but arriving in batches. Post a bit difficult – going the other way too, he says my letters arrive several together. Worrying, I know he is in a very dangerous place. He doesn't say much about it but a lot of wounded coming in here.

We now know why we had to have a hospital here in Nocera. It had to be a place close to the small port. Little ships can steal up the coast to Anzio and take the causalities off the landing beaches and slip down again without the Germans noticing – hopefully.

6th April

Sweetheart darling,
I can see that this letter is going to take a long time getting written. You see I'm using my map case to write on and I've only got to move the pad to see your photograph. I've already spent ten minutes gazing at you. It's all very disturbing – but it's nice. You know, you've no right to be that good-looking, Joy, my sweet.

And of all things, the long-looked for pipe has arrived (with a very sweet note from Mother Barber). It's a good pipe, Joy and I'm very proud of it.

I'm sitting in what was once upon a time a house, but which now serves as my OP (Out Post) which I share with a couple of Yanks. At the present my assistant Sgt. Platt is taking his turn, so I've grabbed the opportunity of scribbling a few lines to you. Old General (Sgt. Platt) is a grand chap. I hope you'll be able to meet him one day soon. I'm sure you'll like him.

The Yanks have just asked, "Would you care for a cup of 'caaaw-feee', Lieutenant?" and are brewing it. So for the time being everything is pretty cheerful. Be happy dear one, and know that I live for you alone.

From your own Tony

He comments on the fact that letters arrive in the most frightfully muddled order. Some were written at the end of February! Mum gets to meet Sergeant Platt because he gets wounded.

Tony has asked me to look up one of his Sergeants, his name is Platt and a Captain he knows, both admitted two days ago. Managed to find them on E3. Very pleased to see me and full of praise for their Lieut.

Tony is delighted that she gets to meet Sergeant Platt. Tony's letter again.

My Dearest,

Glad you went to see Sgt. Platt, and also that you liked him. He is a nice chap isn't he? His code-name, for use over the radio, was 'General' and he is universally known by that name. If you were to call him 'General,' he'd be tickled pink and I'm quite sure he'd be your slave for the rest of his life. I'm getting a bit jealous, by the way, of this ever-growing band of faithful admirers that you are collecting. I don't know what kind of things 'the General' tells you, but you mustn't let him alarm you unduly. (Although, if I know him, I don't think he will).

Honestly, things aren't too bad you know. We're right on the sea-shore and the surroundings are really quite pleasant. The other day, in my efforts to find a good OP, I achieved the distinction of being the nearest man to Rome in the Allied Forces. We've got a cracking command-post just finished, with properly sand-bagged walls and roof, and a table and two chairs inside. Why the damn place is like a mansion. We're thinking of holding a dance in it one of these evenings. I can feel quite safe inside it too, which is a major consideration.

A Frightfully Chummy Business

Another wonderful thrilling letter from you this evening. You make all this nonsense of war seem well worthwhile. To hell with democracy – it's you I'm fighting for.

Have had a letter from another chap who has arrived at the 103rd – one of my signallers. Don't get alarmed my dear one, I shan't ask you to 'adopt' every single one of my soldiers that happen to be wounded. It just happens that these two have been nice enough to write and thank me for the very small things I was able to do for them when they were hit. And I didn't want them to think that they've been forgotten just because they're no longer with us. Besides that, I know damned well that they'll be terribly bucked to think that you've taken the trouble to go and see them. And I know too that you'll make them realise once again that life is worth living.

Quite a successful day on the whole though, and tell Sgt Platt that I think we've finally fixed the G- that got him.

Still grand weather. Trouble is that while everybody else takes every opportunity they get to bask in the sun and develop that attractive tan (which all handsome me must have) I have to crouch in my miserable hole and try and spot the wretched Hun through my carefully arranged camouflage. If this goes on much longer, people will think I'm just a new boy with 'blighty knees'.

What I like about this job is that you can always be doing something, if you want to, and you do have the satisfaction of hitting back. Another thing I like is that you meet so many different people, Infantry, Gunners, Engineers – everybody, and all tumbling over each other to help. Oh it's a frightfully chummy business.

I eventually returned from the OP worn out. Old Bosche paid for it though. I pasted the hell out of him all day and as a result was told that although it was admirable to harass the enemy, I mustn't waste ammunition. On my day off had a wonderful bath this morning in a stream less than a mile from the 'guns'. It was grand, a hot morning and the water was icy cold. Spent the rest of the day sunbathing and lolling about in the sand-dunes. There are flowers all over the dunes and they look like a beautiful mauve carpet. Do you know what they reminded me of – especially the speckled ones? One of those absurd, delicious pieces of underwear that you have. I've an idea that that may be naughty – but it doesn't feel like that my precious.

I think what impresses me the most when reading the diary and the letters is how people took everything in their stride. They simply got on with things even though there was a possibility that death lurked around the corner. Each day could have been their last.

Tony continues to describe his dugout in another letter.

My dear heart,
I'm sitting in the old dugout writing this. There's a hurricane lamp on the table which gives a very mellow, comforting sort of light. The signaller is sitting on my bed-roll and the bugger will insist on talking all the time (excuse me). He's one of those horrible semi-well-educated types – you know, the local clerk you see on Saturday afternoons wearing very pale grey flannels and a bright blue sports coat. Ugh!

Your photograph has its usual place of honour on the wall (flanked, I'm ashamed to add, by various pin-up 'cuties' – not my work, I assure you). Len, my 2 I/C and I have been smoking our pipes solidly for two hours and there's a grand fuzz.

The Naafi arrived today – I got a whole bottle of gin, which I'm saving for a later date, and a bottle of beer which is in front of me now. So you see, sweetheart mine, life isn't too bad. Now and again a piece of Hun nastiness drops a bit near, but all that happens is that a trickle of sand falls from the ceiling.

I feel very close to you these days. It's a wonderful thought and it helps me more than I can say. Goodnight, Joy my own. God keep you safe for me.

From your ever loving husband, Tony

Oscar

Don't think I've told you about Oscar, have I? Oscar is our pet German. He's a hell of a big parachutist, who mans an OP a little way in front of the enemy lines. There happens to be a bulge in our line, and we are in it. That makes us almost parallel with him. But the silly bugger doesn't know it. He's no idea he's being watched. Every now and then he pops up out of his hole, looks around him, struts about a bit and then pops back inside again. We wouldn't hurt Oscar for worlds – he's far too good entertainment. And incidentally he gives away quite a lot of useful information.

Back at the hospital, Mum continues with her duties until one day things take a different turn.

12th April

Supervising serving dinner, fainted. Came round supported by an anxious Bailly – struggled up and assured everyone I was perfectly alright. Bit groggy though. Retired to the office to gather my wits. Have we hit the jackpot first time?

This appears to be the first mention in the diary of any signs that Mum was potentially pregnant.

17th April

Pretty sure – reported to Major (doctor looking after staff health). He agreed possible pregnancy! He was a bit worried, thought I was too thin, 9st too low for 5ft 9ins. Must take care, said I must come off the wards. Suggests light duties in the Mess.

Very happy, very excited – write letter to Tony. He writes back in the same vein and also saying he feels very proud. Anxious to know what happens next. Had to go to a Medical Board in Naples – seen by a senior doctor there. Everything alright and when safe to travel, shall be posted home end of May. Getting marvellous letters from Tony, trying to get some leave, frantic to see me before I am posted. Sad too that we will be parted for a while.

Tony is delighted about the news, but also expresses concern for her. He is very sad that they must be apart, although he is relieved that she is returning to England because he feels that she will be safer there and will be well looked after.

2nd May

My dearest darling,
Any news of your departure yet? I'm very relieved to hear that you've been taken off the wards. Every time I think of you doing the 'morning bumf round' I could laugh my head off. And I'm delighted to hear that you spend a lot of time in the kitchen – just the job, but go easy with those tins.

Tony is desperate to see her before she leaves and manages to get time away from the front. The diary goes into more detail.

14th May Sunday

Tony arrives! Flown down from Anzio, very tanned and very dirty! Oh how lovely to see him! Slept out that night at the flat.

15th May Sorrento

Five bitter sweet days. Tony got some transport from HQ. Everybody being so helpful and kind. Drove into Salerno, then took the scenic route around the coast to Sorrento. Very lovely warm evening with the sun setting behind the mountains, turning them beautiful colours. The sea very calm and blue. Almost dark when we reach the YMCA – given sandwiches and coffee. Retire to our own room in the town's major building, large and airy with a little balcony. Stood looking out over this very beautiful romantic town. Spent two more very pleasant days exploring the town, not doing anything much, just so happy being together.

We are haunted by the agony of the parting so soon to come though.

Spent a day in Naples. Took the long route around the bay, spectacular views but rather bumpy, damaged road. Did some shopping, lunch at the Club, back to Sorrento. Sat on the balcony watching the sun set, listening to Neapolitan music coming from somewhere below. So sad.

19th May

Back to the hospital, and Tony leaves to go back to Anzio. Afraid there were tears, oh so many at this parting. How long will it be before we meet again? Tony thinks not so very long. When the fighting is over in Italy he says the forces will be sent home on much deserved leave and retraining for next move. Must hang onto that thought and look forward. After all, we planned this move – we so badly wanted to start our family, want to be young with our children growing up, we said!

20th May

Transferred to the 104th Base Hospital, to await my journey home to England. Sad farewell to friends, we've been through a lot together, good and bad times but mostly good on the whole.
Sisters' Mess 104th rather splendid villa and very comfortable, great improvement on our place at Nocera.

23rd May

The British and American troops launch an offensive from Anzio beachhead. Tony was involved in this.

24th May

My Birthday. Am twenty five!
Proceed to docks complete with kit. Board the EI NIL, rather battered cargo ship converted to hospital ship. Sail out from Bay of Naples at sundown. Still a lot of damaged ships and wrecks around. Last view of Naples is a mass of twinkling lights.

Home Again

2nd June

Sailed up the Clyde. How green the countryside is!

3rd June

We disembark. Fortunately an orderly to handle my luggage, and got me to the London train. Arrived Euston late evening. Met by mother & sister, (had managed to phone home from Scotland). The city was full of Yanks & all the hotels were booked up. We queued up with everyone else to try and get accommodation. I was dressed in my uniform, the grey and scarlet. One of the Officials saw my uniform and took us to the front of the queue. He managed to find us accommodation.

4th June

Arrive home.

Mum stays with her parents in Kent. Her part in the war may be over but not for Tony. He remains in Italy. Now we can continue to build up a picture of the war from his point of view though the many letters that he writes. I believe Mum kept them all.

Tony and Joy, Italy 1944

Joy 1944

Tony

Italy

Tony has not been able to write for a while as he is involved in all the activity at Anzio and the surrounding area.

6th June

I'm desperately sorry, but I'm afraid it is a fact that you've got to face, that when you want to know how and where I am, that's just the time that I simply can't write letters to you. During the past few exciting eventful days, the fact that I had no opportunity to write to you was the only cloud on my horizon.

Well, here I am my darling. It's been the most wonderful experience. I've fought in successful battles before, but never anything quite like this. It was a rout. The longest we stayed in any place was sixty hours. For the rest, it was a question of swarming along the roads, jumping out of the vehicles to pop off a few rounds and then off again. My platoon was with the leading infantry battalion, and we actually were the first people to reach the River Tiber. We're out of the battle now and this afternoon I'm going to have a look around Rome.

And they've landed in France this morning.* You know, although it's foolish to be over optimistic, one can't help hoping. Please God that this nonsense may stop soon. And that I may come back to you as soon as possible.

*The D-Day Landings

8th June Rome

Went to Rome the day before yesterday and we all got unbelievably tight. My God it was monumental. Of course at that time we hadn't had the place long. Today the city is out of bounds and by tomorrow no doubt there will be notices all over the place saying 'Out of bounds to all ranks' and 'Officers only' and all that kind of nonsense. But on Tuesday it was wonderful. After quarter of an hour the jeep was smothered with flowers and everywhere we went we were cheered. It was a wonderful experience.

Rome is a lovely city. There is literally no comparison between Rome and Naples. The streets are broad and clean and of course there are magnificent buildings. There doesn't seem to be much in the shops and what there is seems to be absurdly expensive. Anyway half of them were closed. The people are well dressed and positively clean! There are some very good hotels too, still every bit as good as some of the first-class London hotels.

Tony has some special news in July. He has been promoted to Captain.

21st July

I've been promoted to Captain. Apparently I've been a Captain for the last three weeks but nobody ever tells me anything, so I wouldn't know. All I hope is that they've been paying me for it since then.

Had two letters this evening – one from you and one from Mother. Yours was started on the 13th, finished on the 16th and posted on the 17th – which in my opinion is pretty snappy work on the part of the APO.

We really are getting down to it, my sweet, at this place. Tonight will be the third night-exercise this week. And we don't get any extra rest the next day either. Italy is particularly hot and the hotter it gets, the smells become correspondingly worse. And the flies – Africa had nothing on this place. Oh for England, home and beauty - that's you my dear.

Tony goes on to say how much he misses Joy and hopes that the war won't go on for too much longer.

Joy goes to visit the in-laws and Tony mentions his concerns about the V1 flying bombs, known as 'doodlebugs', flying over Kent to bomb London.

23rd July

This flying bomb affair sounds perfectly bloody awful to me. Thank God that you're out of it. Hope that Mother and Father Barber are quite safe.

30th July

We held a race meeting yesterday afternoon and grand fun it was. Very like those organised by the RATD at Chateaudun. Mule races, donkey races – damn funny they were too. I rode in the Officers' race and came third. The horses were quite good, but of course we'd never seen them before. The track was terribly dusty and very short – in fact it was one long corner. Anyway, everybody enjoyed it and it was decided unanimously to have another one next month.

Afterwards we entertained our guests to tea in the camp, a cocktail party in our billet and a dance in the Mess. They were all Sisters from the 100th and the 72nd who live about fifteen miles away. Those girls were certainly a grand bunch and we had a first class party. Everybody 'mucked in' and there was nothing that even I could disapprove of.

In August, he starts instructing on a series of courses which keep him extremely busy.

12th August

My feet have hardly touched the ground. Just a small cloud of dust rushing madly in five different directions – that has been Capt. Case, The Sherwood Foresters for the last three days. And work on Saturday afternoon too! Horror!

14th August

Another letter from you this evening. Thank you my sweet – you write grand letters. I simply wallow in all the little personal details you tell me. I can picture you oh so clearly – you're very near to me all the time.

It's been so hot today – I feel absolutely beat. Am now sitting in my bedroom wearing the very minimum with a glass of lemonade at my elbow. Dinner was a scream tonight. It was an excellent meal, we are fed extraordinarily well here, but the sight of fifteen odd Officers sitting round a table all mumbling and cursing and hugging at their ties and perspiring freely was really too funny for words. Tried to get cool afterwards by drinking our coffee on the balcony. But the balcony overlooks one of the filthiest streets in one of the filthiest villages imaginable. Added to that there were about forty Italian children, all screaming and playing around in the dirt, and the smell was even worse than usual. I can't remember it being as bad as this even in Africa at the worst.

I don't think I've told you about my billet. It's a nice room – usually quite cool, and very comfortably furnished with easy chairs, a sofa, bedside tables and lamp and a chest of drawers. And there's electric light and hot water (not running, though). Real luxury, my dear. The two old ladies who live in the house 'mother me' quite nicely. Besides providing flowers and fruit for the room, they also do my laundry very efficiently. The other night they insisted on taking my temperature 'cos I looked a bit pale! I respond with the occasional bar of chocolate and we get on very well.

Good night my beloved wife. God bless you and our child and God keep you safe for me.

From your own Tony

The weather is extremely hot and life goes on much as usual, in fact he complains that it is extremely monotonous at times. He spends a lot of time dreaming and planning for their future and becomes quite pensive. He writes,

The very fact that you are going to hold this letter in your hands gives me much satisfaction. I could go on writing the most awful nonsense just for the sake of sending something to you.

23rd August

I'm in an awful state this evening – quite literally I don't know whether I'm coming or going. We got up at midnight last night and didn't get back 'til eleven this morning, having dashed around the countryside in pitch darkness for about five hours. I've been asleep ever since and am now completely disorganised. Oh hell! I'm sure I had a letter from you yesterday, but damned if I can find it now. Think I must have left it in the pocket of a shirt sent to the laundry.

3rd September

We've decided that during the next course it would be a good thing to take the students to a battlefield and go over the battle with them on the ground. Salerno is the most convenient place. So when this course ends we're going down to Ravello for a few days to have a look

round. It should be very pleasant, but I suppose it will mean that I'll have to do a lot more work.

16th September

There's a dance on in the Mess again tonight but somehow I'm not in the right mood. There are only Sisters there and it always makes me sad when I see a scarlet and grey uniform, let alone dance with one.

The course turns out to be a huge success. He goes on to describe it in more detail.

12th October

*We were billeted in a huge school and of course there wasn't a stick of furniture in the place. However it was plumb in the middle of the town which was convenient. I think the trip was a decided success – socially as well as instructionally. One day we spent with the gunners was a dead loss, but the TEWT (*Tactical Exercise Without Troops) *on the battlefield was a great success.*

The students fairly lapped it up – and it was extremely interesting for me too. Actually it was the last battle I took part in before I packed up. There was a holiday spirit about the whole affair, and as usual at the end of a course the students did their level best to get the instructors sewn up. We had a couple of very good parties at the club.

Arrived back here at four o'clock this evening to find three letters from you waiting for me. Having been without mail for four days I was just about panting for them. And guess what – the parcel containing the photo frame and the tobacco pouch has turned up at long last, battered but intact. Thank you my sweet one, they are grand. And the photographs – I'm so proud of them. You know, that funny old wife of mine really is a very beautiful woman.

16th October

Have spent today down in Amalfi with the others. Started off to walk down dressed in the nearest I can manage to civilian clothes. Got a lift in a jeep however, crowded with Officers, belonging to a man dressed in grey flannels and a tennis shirt with whom I shared the front seat rather intimately! We chatted away about this, that and the other and I gave bent to a good old English oath when we nearly disappeared over a five hundred foot precipice. I've just met him again this evening – and he's all dressed up in the full paraphernalia of a Brigadier. He's a nice bloke though. I must have looked a wee bit embarrassed 'cause he laughed and apologised for taking an unfair advantage.

Spent the morning on the beach. It was grand. The water was lovely and warm and it was almost too hot to lie and sunbathe on the beach. Not bad for the middle of October.

Later, he walks back, freshens up and has a smoke.

I smoke a quiet cigarette on my balcony looking over perhaps the most beautiful scene in the world. So here I am feeling all clean, powdered and unutterably lonely. A good day I suppose it has been. But it means nothing – literally nothing – because you are not with me here, Joy my sweet. The other part, the part of me which matters, is always with you.

He finishes the letter in his usual way by declaring his love.

In his next letter he remarks about the conditions and weather.

Winter has come and with a vengeance. Today its been so cold it just isn't true. And now my hands are frozen and I can hardly hold my pen, let alone control it. There's snow on the hills and if it goes on like this it will soon be down here too. You know those leather jerkins that are issued to infantry? I've had the sleeves and collar of an OR's greatcoat put on to one and also a lining. Grand and warm it is and generally rather snappy, though I'm not quite sure that you'd approve – it's a wee bit 'Eighth Armyish'. But we mustn't sneer at the desert mice any longer – the Foresters are part of them nowadays.

I love the idea of your last letter being written on the rather unstable support of D/J's behind. I hardly think that kind of thing shows the respect due to a person of such importance.

What is happening now, Joy my beloved? I suppose you will be going into hospital soon. I'm completely in the dark about it all – I'm quite prepared for a telegram to arrive any minute now and tell me it was all over days ago.

7th November

A baby girl is born, Josephine, my sister. Tony receives the news by cablegram. He is of course very excited and over the moon. He finds it difficult to put into words what he feels but then expresses it as,

That first crashing burst of happiness and it's all so huge, so wonderful, so glorious, marvellous – it's all the words like that. I'm sort of living in a maze of superlatives. The size of it! It's such a big thing that's happened to us – its lifted me right up to heaven and I can't get my feet back onto earth again.

People have been calling all morning to congratulate me and send their best wishes to you – they're nearly as excited about it as I am.

In later letters his delight is tinged with guilt and helplessness that he can't be there with them as he feels he should be. He's also concerned for her safety.

15th November

And now, my sweet, I'm going to fuss again. It's about those wretched rockets. Seriously, darling, what is it all

about? Are they as horrible as one would imagine from what one reads? If they are a nuisance in the slightest degree, you must promise me to go back to Derby as soon as you can. I've no doubt that sooner or later you will be press-ganged into going back in order to parade the 'Pride of the Cases' before her admiring relatives. Don't stay in Kent any longer than you need, dear heart, if there is the slightest danger.

However, Joy stays in Kent a little while longer.

28th November

There's a cinema show for Officers this evening. The film was the 'Desert Song' and very entertaining it was. Lots of people rushing about the Sahara on horses and suddenly bursting into song at the most unlikely times. And the most immaculate natives. I began to wonder if my ideas concerning North Africa were inaccurate, but somehow I don't think so. And the way in which the story was twisted about to make it topical is nobody's business. Believe it or not, the Nazis had crept into this story somehow or other.

The latest craze in the Mess is for darts. We get quite excited over it. In Depot HQ there are two Officers' Messes, ours for instructors, and the other one for the permanent staff of the depot HQ. We have the most intense dart matches against each other for a cup made out of a 4 lb jam tin. We're also lucky in having two good pianists and we spend a lot of time singing – we're getting quite good. Of course, as the evening wears on the songs become more doubtful.

10th December

I haven't told you that the new course had already been in operation a week. I was all set to be terribly browned off and bored but I've got such a nice set of chaps to instruct that I have to admit that it isn't as bad as I expected. They really are a grand lot. It's queer how they vary from one course to another.

In addition to my normal work I've been given the job of producing an Information Room. I've spent literally hours putting up maps, cutting photographs out of the 'Sphere' and sticking them up. It takes every minute of my spare time, but I'm not complaining, in fact I rather welcome it.

1945

A new year and this also brings new opportunities. Tony decides to apply to the SBS (Special Boat Service).

14th January

There's one thing I might as well tell you about now, rather than later. My main object in going down to Bari last week was to have an interview with the CO of the Special Boat Service. I had it, was accepted, and am due to go within the next week or so. It involves parachuting.

Now let's get this straight my beloved Joy, it will take me several months to train and several more probably, before I go on an operation. I am not at liberty to leave whenever I like. And I'm going into this with my eyes wide open and I know what I'm doing. And I'd rather do that, far rather than lead an infantry platoon again. And those were the two alternatives. I had to get out of this place. I suppose it will be too much to hope that you will be as glad about it as I am. But know this, my darling wife, I shall be happy and contented (as far as is possible when I'm away from you) and my conscience will be easy. And you will have the consolation of knowing that your husband really is doing a worthwhile job again.

He writes again the very next day.

I've realised already what an extraordinarily stupid letter it was that I sent you yesterday. What I mean is, that having ticked you off for worrying and having told you that there will never be any need for it, I follow up with the news that I'm going to leave a safe and comparatively comfortable job in order to go and jump out of aeroplanes. So I'm writing this early in the hope that it will arrive the same day as the other.

He goes on to explain that there are many people where he is who have done very little, whereas there are thousands of people who are doing far more than their share and he wants to do his bit too. He writes,

And I don't want Josephine to remember that her father, a young and fit man, spent a long time merely training other people to go and fight. And I want you to be able to be proud of me. And a lot of other things like that.

Tony waits for his orders. He has time on his hands and goes to the hospital theatre and sees the film, 'Going My Way', starring Bing Crosby.

A grand film. What did upset me though was that at the end of the film, I discovered that about fifty odd Hun prisoners – unescorted as far as I could see – had been allowed to watch the show. Apparently it's the usual thing.

I've made up my mind to become interested in ballet. Does that please you? I'm busy learning all I can about

it. There's a book called, 'Balletmania', and I would be very grateful if you could get hold of it for me.

He asks after Josephine and is literally pining for news of the pair of them. In his next letter he states,

This is a bad place for me to be in – too many people waiting to go home and all chattering about it so excitedly. I'm beginning to wonder how much longer I can last out. The sooner I get some real work to do the better.

While he is still waiting for his orders to come through, he at long last manages to meet up with Freddie.

11th February

Joy, my darling wife,
I've seen Freddie – and of course he's everything you've said he was and more. I was only with him for a short time, but dearest, I did like him. And his face is the same shape and colouring as yours (just a hint of freckles!) and he's got your eyes and mouth – oh it was almost heart breaking. It's been a filthy afternoon – simply pouring with rain and the poor chap had taken refuge in his tent. When I found him, he was just about to retire to his bed. I think he was just about as nervous as I was. I've realised now that, as is usual when I'm nervous, I chatter away like hell. Promise to tell me what his

opinion of me is. My God, it was almost as big an ordeal as the first time I went to Rosedale. I thought perhaps it would be best if I didn't stay too long the first time, so we arranged to meet next Thursday evening. Shall try to get hold of a vehicle from somewhere. Somehow, I think we shall get on rather well together.

Back in England, the war was still raging and now the V2s, the German flying bombs, were flying over Kent to attack London. Yet again, Tony voices his concern for Joy's and Josephine's safety.

Look here, my precious Joy, there's been talk in the papers of more bombs over Southern England. Don't you think if they're going to start a last minute piece of nastiness, it would be better for you not to live in Kent? I suppose you've realised by now that I shall natter about that at every opportunity that arises. But seriously I would be happier if I could know that you were safe.

Below is the story that Mum told me of that time.

The bomb that dropped

With the bombs flying overhead, being bombed was a real danger so when Josephine was asleep, she would be placed between the strongest wall in the house and the sofa.

You never heard these bombs coming until it was too late. One particular day my Auntie Eileen was washing up in the kitchen. Mum came into the room and Eileen had just taken her hands out of the washing up bowl and turned to talk to Mum when suddenly, there was a terrible explosion and all the glass from the window shattered into the washing up bowl. If Eileen had still had her hands in it, they would have been cut to pieces. A bomb had dropped short of its target and landed a few miles away.

Another bomb story that occurred in the early part of the war was told to me by Eileen. Mum had come back home on leave. At this time she was still nursing in England. One afternoon, they were all sitting round a table playing cards when the air siren sounded.

They should have rushed off to the shelter immediately but having become rather blasé about these things, they decided to ignore it. Mum had just gone off to make cocoa for everybody when 'CRASH', there was an almighty explosion and the latch from the front door blew off, leaving the door hanging. My Uncle Rex and Patch, the family dog, got into a terrible tangle of arms and legs as they both dived under the table.

My grandfather was particularly angry because the bomb had shattered all the glass in the greenhouses and they spent days picking up all the fragments.

As Eileen said, "You just learnt to live with these things."

Meanwhile, back in Italy Tony does not meet up with Freddie as arranged because he now receives the long awaited orders to join the SBS. He is then involved in a frenzy of packing and saying many goodbyes.

21st February Terrible Journey

Joy, my dearest darling,
As far as I can remember it's exactly a week since I last wrote to you. I'm desperately sorry to leave you so long without a letter – but it really was unavoidable. And brother – what a week. I'll tell you all about it. It will take at least two letters, so perhaps that will atone for the long gap. I may say the thought of you waiting for letters that never arrive has nearly driven me frantic.

All day Thursday was spent trying to say goodbye to everybody but it was quite impossible. There are six different battalions and a large HQ.

On Friday morning I packed. You should see the kit I've collected. I had a small party with my intimate friends from Depot HQ and pushed off to Caserta just before tea.

I arrived there at about five o'clock, and then began a really hair-raising journey by train. To begin with I had with me a very large and heavy valise, a large wooden box, which I could hardly lift and another tin one which was almost as heavy. Added to that was my leather grip, my small pack and my equipment. And nobody but me to cart it about. However, while waiting for the train at Caserta I met two other Officers who were travelling light and they helped me. We eventually got on the right train – mind you we had been instructed to stand on the wrong side and at the wrong end of the station. We got a compartment to ourselves, and by hanging blankets over the broken windows and sticking candles in odd corners managed to make ourselves fairly comfortable.

The train didn't actually go to Foggia where I was making for but only about five miles away from it, so at about two o'clock in the morning I had to change. Just imagine – pitch darkness, all that kit – a strange station and I didn't know where or when my train left and it seemed that neither did anybody else. However I made it, and arrived in Foggia at half past four.

Wandered around the town until I found the Transit Hotel, got a room and slept there for a couple of hours. Having had a hot bath and some breakfast, I felt much better, and telephoned to the new unit. At about half-past ten, a jeep arrived for me and I started off again. It was eighty miles and took about two and a half hours to the Unit Rear HQ. It's in the most remarkable place. A queer little town perched right high up in the mountains and overlooking the sea. And bitterly cold, a biting wind all the time and it started to snow a little. Got myself established in the Mess there and was welcomed quite warmly. Luckily there's a chap there I know quite well.

On Sunday morning I was told that the Adjutant wanted to see me in Bari. So off I set again - one hundred and twenty miles this time in a fifteen CWT.

Arrived there just before tea and met the Adjutant who told me quite frankly that he only wanted to have a look at me and also that I was to see the acting second in command the next day. Had dinner at the Imperial with some chaps from the 46th Division and spent the night in a flat in the town owned by the SBS.

27th February A Virtuous Life

Joy, my darling,
Apart from a compulsory and most uncomfortable bare-back ride on a mule this morning, I have nothing to do. And so naturally I've jumped at the opportunity of writing to you. Quite seriously, this letter-writing is going to be rather a problem. There literally isn't a table in the place to write at. And I've run out of ink and can't get any more. They really are the most casual people imaginable here – there is no attempt at organisation. In most respects that's rather pleasant – at least it is un-military which is a delightful change. And it certainly seems to produce good results. The house in which I sleep has a sun-roof and that is where I am now, using my map case and my knees as rather an unsteady desk.

The weather has been wonderful for the last three days and I'm sitting up here clad only in slacks, shirt and pullover. The house is surrounded by olive trees and orange and lemon trees with the fruit on them. About four hundred yards away, the sea, that absurdly blue colour, is lapping up against a nice clean beach, and altogether it's rather a lovely spot. And all I can do is sit and think of how heavenly it would be if I could share it with you.

You just wouldn't believe the virtuous life I've been leading lately. Last night I went to bed at ten o'clock but every other night I've been sound asleep by nine. And the exercise! PT every morning and the rest of the day just as strenuous. I'm glowing with ruddy 'ealth and feeling wonderfully fit again.

There are now nine Officers down here, three other re-enforcements like myself and the others old hands. We have decided to form a Mess. At the present that consists of taking our rations down to a café a mile away and eating there. So far we've lived almost entirely on macaroni, spaghetti and risotto, but I must say I like it. Oh, and eggs of course. It's the dirtiest, scruffiest, dingiest place imaginable, run by the inevitable Italian who has spent twenty odd years in America. He is helped by an incredibly aged woman who croaks like a frog and is really rather a dear.

Nearly every letter from Tony describes his longing to see Joy and Josephine. Every letter he declares his love and his hopes to see them soon but as time goes on, that dream seems to slip further and further away. His letters become more and more desperate. He declares that soon he should be able to return to England, it is just a question of when.

Joy is still living at home with her parents but things are not going well between them and Tony expresses concerns for her. She decides to go up to Derby to live with her parents-in-law. She still anticipates that Tony might be coming home soon. Meanwhile, he is busy training.

6th March Training

I was told to start my training. I packed up and had an eighty mile ride on a three tonner over nearly vertical mountains and round hair-raising corners. This place is on the sea, very pleasant, but still cold and absolutely desolate and isolated. We are living in summer villas, but there is not a stick of furniture in the place and no Mess. I am writing this on my bed wrapped up in a blanket by the light of a candle. The nearest place is a small village with a couple of wine bars about five miles away. Strangely enough I like it. Started my training today and was thoroughly interested – lots of new weapons and things to learn about. But I've got to get fit too, which is going to be a bit of a strain.

There's a grand set of chaps here – both Officers and men, some of them quite mad and others exactly the opposite. But it's a real pleasure to be with them. I'm satisfied, my sweet Joy, that I've done the right thing, and I'm as happy as I can be while I'm away from you. And when the time comes for a spot of action I shall be very confident – which is always a great help.

They are making us work extraordinarily hard down here but it's interesting and I'm thoroughly enjoying it.

Parachute Course

A letter dated 20th of March informs Joy that he has just completed a Parachutist Course. He writes,

Made my first jump a week ago yesterday – and dislocated my bloody shoulder. So here I am in the 98th.

In his next letter he goes into more detail.

23rd March 98th General Hospital

Joy my beloved,
I really will try and tell you what I've been doing in the last few days. You were quite right, of course, it was a parachute course – down at Givia, about twenty five miles south of Bari. Think I've described the camp and the general administration there in other letters, but in case I haven't, one word will sum it up – bloody. The instruction however, by RAF NCOs was excellent. They were a first class music-hall comedy turn in their own right. Our squad instructor's name was Tingle – and we were 'Tingle's Terrors'. He had us in fits of laughter most of the time. Most of them have done two hundred jumps. The preliminary ground training takes five days – a few odd lectures and training films, but above all bags of work on the various devices and lots of PT. They had us jumping through holes in the platforms, off moving trolleys, rolling around in sandpits, swinging on huge great swings and God

knows what. I discovered muscles in my body which I didn't know existed.

At last we were ready for the first jump – and then the weather broke. For three days the wind was too strong for safe parachuting and for three days we hang around getting more and more excited, depressed or frightened (as it affected you personally). I don't remember feeling anything very much one way or the other. At last the great day arrived. Got up at 5.30, no breakfast, off to the packing-sheds to draw chutes and then straight to the air field. There wasn't any hanging around – thank God- and soon we were off (in a Wellington). I was the very first person to jump. I really wasn't frightened – I was far too concerned about making a good exit. In the Wellington you go through a hole in the floor. My main worry at the last minute was that I should fall out before he told me to go.

At last he said, "Go!" And I went.

Darling, it's the most wonderful sensation. I can honestly say I enjoyed it. The most exhilarating rush and then that wonderful feeling when you realise that she's opened and there you are gently floating down in utter and complete silence. I let out a yell of delight and was promptly ticked off by an instructor on the ground (through a megaphone). More tomorrow darling Joy.

All my love is yours forever. Tony

In his next letter, we learn more about the dislocated shoulder.

It was entirely my own fault. I was enjoying it so much, it was so easy and I was so confident that I forgot all I had been taught and – crash! I'd landed. The doctor out in the 'dropping zone' fixed me up temporally and whipped me away down here in an ambulance straight away.

Tony later develops a temperature and has to spend some time in the hospital. He gets well looked after.

27th March

I think the SBS is rather a favourite unit here. There are three of us together in one small ward and we get looked after very well. Bags of tinned fruit and eggs, two bottles of beer a day and a lot of whisky every evening.

In a later letter he asks after Josephine and writes,

It's an odd experience being the father of a child you've never seen. It's like knowing that there is a new part of our love and yet not knowing what it is like.

Josephine is now five months old and growing rapidly.
Joy has expressed feelings of being lonely and Tony writes with concern in his next letter.

9th April

I'm still a bit worried about your being lonely. Don't like to think of you having to rely on visits to the cinema with Uncle Tim for entertainment, though he is undoubtedly a very charming and entertaining person. If I could think of any of my friends who were still in Derby, I would write to them and introduce you. But I don't know though!

Important news my sweet. I have been selected for a Regular Commission. A form arrived today asking me if I still wanted one, if I was still A1 and if you were a German (or something of the sort). After a very little hesitation I filled it in and so there we are.

Sweet Joy, I too am convinced it is the right thing for me to do. I don't think either of us have any illusions about what it will mean. Let's face it, it may even mean more partings for us and our having to be apart again. But not for long. When all this is over I shan't let you out of my sight again. I shall drag you all over the place with me, even to India! I pray with all my heart and soul that you will never regret having married a soldier.

Not many of Joy's letters have survived. We can only guess at her thoughts and feelings by reading the responses in Tony's letters. But her response to Tony's news does survive.

Dearest Darling Tony,
Just received your letter written on the 9th – very pleased with your news re the Regular Commission. You have no idea, such a load off my mind. Since

they started this special selection business, I've been in a cold sweat, not that I have ever doubted your abilities, but just because our future was swinging so to speak!

She goes on to declare her love and express how much she wants him home.

Now to return to Tony's letters.

15th April

Like a complete nincompoop, I forgot to thank you for the tobacco that was included in your parcel. I do so now, sweet Joy. Did somebody tell you to buy Well's Cut Golden Bar, may I ask, or was it just your own good taste? Anyway you couldn't have chosen a better brand – I'm the envy of the Mess.

We have quite a pleasant Mess here, about forty minutes ride from Bari, in an olive grove and near the main road. It is a large wooden hut, fairly comfortably furnished. The food is excellent and drink in quite good supply. We are living in tents, but I have one to myself and the weather is becoming very warm.

The local town is a typical small Italian port but rather more pleasant and cleaner than the average.

No air-mail letters from you recently, but today there arrived a sea-mail letter which had only been posted a week ago – which is pretty good going.

17th April Accident in the Harbour

About ten days ago there was the most ghastly accident in the harbour at Bari. A ship carrying a cargo of bombs blew up. The hospital must be nearly two miles from the docks but I was quite prepared for bits of it to fall down, so colossal was the explosion. The casualties – Italian and British – were frightful. Somebody did an excellent job of work at the hospitals, the reception was first class. I had a very busy afternoon putting people to bed, washing them and generally making them comfortable.

The explosion in the harbour happened on 9th April and involved the ship SS Charles Henderson. The Liberty Ship exploded and sank when her cargo of 2,000 tons of bombs detonated. There were 360 killed and 1,730 wounded in the port.*

24th April

I've been doing a course on explosives and demolitions under the instruction of our expert. We've had great fun – lots of colossal bangs. Scared the Italians out of their wits but fortunately did no damage. That, and the odd spot of PT has kept me fairly well occupied during the day.

Tony now joins a special unit called 'M' Squadron.

* Wikipedia List of shipwrecks in April 1945

26th April

At last I have been able to persuade them to give me some work to do. I've been nattering away steadily for the last few days and I've worn them down gradually. Within the next few days I am to go and join my squadron. This being a 'special unit', I can't tell you where we are operating. But I assure you, there is no need for worry on your part. I'm very glad to be going to M Squadron, they are very well thought of, and I know some of the Officers quite well.

Was it in my last letter that I let go about parties in this country? Well – I now declare my intentions concerning them. Last night the navy asked us down to 'have a quiet drink' in their wardroom. We arrived to find a 'do' in full swing. And who should be there but an infantry subaltern and a Sister who had just been married. It was very nearly too much for me.

Special Request

Then on 27th April Tony makes a very special request.

Darling,
I've got rather an extraordinary request to make. It's slightly embarrassing too – though God knows why. You see I've had to destroy a lot of your letters today and the task of choosing which ones to keep was quite impossible. So will you please write a special one for me – one to keep with me always. Don't hurry, and don't

try – just let it happen. And darling, if it has to be at the expense of one of your normal letters – I'd rather not have it. You see the letters that you write to me so often are more precious to me – they're invaluable. Hope you understand all this and why I do want a special one.

To destroy Joy's letters must have been devastating for Tony and very difficult for him to do. Her letters were a life-line to him, his link to his family, to a normal existence and his anchor in life. Joy and his daughter are his life, what he fights for and lives for.

Joy writes,

About that special letter darling, I will write one dearest but not this evening. I shall have to be alone and quiet, so quiet that I will hear your voice and feel your touch, then my darling I can write those things that I would like to say when I am tightly held in your arms, words for you alone.

Whether Joy wrote the special letter or not, is unknown. It has not been found among the numerous letters in the box.

Meanwhile, out in the world, Europe is now in an uproar of ecstatic celebration.

4th May Friday Joy's letter

My darling,
We are so thrilled about the news. Quite honestly, we

are nearly off our heads! Mother came home the other evening and woke me up (had gone to bed at 8pm) to tell me Italy had surrendered, said she was going to put a hot-water bottle in your bed!?!?

Derby is looking very festive, Union Jacks everywhere and all sorts of bunting and what not. All the children waving little flags and everybody wearing red, white and blue posies!

Auntie Kathleen (Tony's Aunt) and I went shopping this afternoon, didn't buy anything but tried hard! Wanted an odd skirt (for VE day) but couldn't find anything I liked. Besides, my bottom still seems to be too big! Have been wondering (and worrying just a little) whether you got going on your job as it was what you wanted so much. I hope you did.

Josephine even more wonderful. She sits up alone now, but she hasn't produced a tooth yet.

I am yours forever, Joy

7th May Tony's letter.

And so it's all over - in Europe. It's no good – I just can't work up any enthusiasm or excitement. I just feel flat. All that's happened is that my impatience to get back to you and Josephine has increased more than ever. Far more important to me than any news is the fact that waiting for me in the Mess when I got back, were some lovely letters from you and the studio portrait of you and Josephine.

Saturday (post marked 7th May) Joy's letter

Tony, my dearest darling,
It's been raining very hard all day – so depressing to be shut up in the house and I am especially disappointed because I wanted to plant some more seeds today! I love pottering about in the garden. I spend hours at it now. In the afternoons Josephine sits up in her pram and watches me. She talks away in her own sweet fashion, laughs and gurgles at the birds and my bobbing head!

It has been announced on the wireless that the Germans have decided to surrender. Issy (Tony's Aunt) phoned within five minutes of the announcement to tell me to keep my ears pinned back! Everybody seems to think that Churchill will broadcast the good news any minute now!

8th May Victory in Europe Day

VE Plus one! My darling,
I didn't write yesterday, it was such a busy and exciting day, I never had time! Derwent Ave is a mass of flags from end to end. We had one medium-sized Union Jack flying from the landing window; rather a poor effort compared to Mrs. Smith's which looks about eight feet square! And most of the houses have at least half a dozen sticking up all around! Not to mention V illuminations and flood lighting!
I have just come in from the garden and eaten my solitary supper. Shall go to bed when I have finished

this letter. Lots of the seeds I planted are beginning to come up. Shall have the garden a blaze of flowers, I hope, for your welcome home.

Daddy took a snap of Josephine to-day with your rugger cap on her head – she did look funny but she was delighted. She has been longing to 'get a hold of' that cap, it's the colour that fascinates her I think. She always looks up at it and smiles when we go into your bedroom. Can you tell me <u>when</u> you will be coming home or are things still being very 'hush-hush'?

Haven't had a letter from you for ages, over a week I think. I am dying to know what you have been doing. God bless you my darling. You are always in my heart. Joy

Doubt and Uncertainty

Now that the war has ended in Europe, things might have settled down but this was not the case as Tony remarks in his next letter. He admits that if it was not for Joy, he would go completely haywire.

10th May

Far from settling things, as far as we are concerned, the end of the war seems to have made everything extraordinarily infinite. Before the end, we did at least know what we were doing. Now, nobody has the vaguest idea.

The Mess is very crowded these days – there are over thirty Officers here and we only have one hut. Afraid I've lost my taste for regimental soldering.

However, Tony's mood picks up again and his later letters are more cheerful.

18th June It's a Grand Life

It's just as lovely here as ever. The weather is perfect, wonderful blue sky and a blazing sun. The beach is grand and the sea very warm – almost too warm. What is so nice about it is that if you get bored with the sea and the sands, there are lovely woods and hills which come right down to the edge of the beach.

We have a swimming parade at 6.30 in the morning, breakfast at 7.30, and the inspection parade at 9. Then at 10.30 there is PT and from then until lunch time we play base-ball or go boating. The dress for the day is a bathing costume (or shorts), gym shoes and nothing else. Altogether it's a grand life and I'm feeling tons better already. If only I could have you with me.

It's a very simple life we lead, but very healthy. I haven't seen a newspaper for four days - neither have I had a drink stronger than tea.

Yesterday I took my patrol out in one of our little motor-boats – they're called 'dories'. We visited a small island about fifteen miles off the coast and it took all day. Took food with us, went ashore and had a swim and a meal there. It's absolutely uninhabited except for swarms and swarms of birds, but it's very quiet and peaceful. From the looks of one end of it, it has been used by the RAF for practice bombing. I was a bit worried that they might suddenly decide to use it again – but however, all was well. We had taken some explosive with us and on the way back we did a little illegal fishing by dropping our home-made bombs overboard. We hoped to kill a few fish. We got so many, that the whole squadron had fish for lunch today! God knows what kind they were but they tasted good.

He goes on to say that it all sounds grand but,

Everything seems so empty and meaningless. I want to be with my wife and child. Going home to you is the light at the end of this rather dark tunnel through which I've been travelling for this last year.

22nd June A Posh Do

Had such a grand letter from you today – the first for nearly a week but that is because we are so far away from the base. You sound wonderfully happy, beloved Joy and I'm terribly, terribly glad. It's done me a whole power of good.

We are still living the same idle aimless rather pleasant life. The sea has been 'up' for the last two days which has put an end to our long-range boating. But we've had grand fun in the canoes. The breakers turned me over more times than I can remember this morning.

Yesterday evening we were invited to the home of one of the two leading families in the district. You'd have died of laughing, my dear. We sat in an 'inner circle' in the drawing room and sipped very primly at some excellent wine. Behind us, and around us in an outer circle, if you see what I mean, sat all the servants and family retainers from the butler downwards to the gardener's small son.

As the evening wore on, there was a series of alarming grunts which quite startled me – but it was only the older ones falling asleep and beginning to snore. The old man has the right idea about most things. The mother is a complete nonentity. The elder daughter is at the University of Naples and spoke passable French. But darling, her hair in a bun and spectacles, positively too studious. I could just imagine her thick woollen, sensible underwear. The younger one was overcome by giggles any time anybody spoke to her.

All rather trying, but extremely amusing.
Goodnight, sweet Joy
All my love, Tony

Back at home, Joy voices a slight inclination to go back to the QAs but it is just a passing thought as she writes,

26th June

A very cheerful letter from you this morning, what a

lovely time you are having, sounds like a boy scouts' paradise!

Frances is on her way home for twenty eight days leave then off to Burma. I wish I was going with her. Honestly Tony, with all my grousing about the life, I am once again longing for a hospital ward and some good hard work to do. You needn't worry though, I couldn't bear to part with Josephine. She is the strongest anchor I have ever had!

Tony is sad to hear that Joy wants to go back to the QAs (3rd July) He also understands that there are tensions living with his parents and that the situation is not ideal.

Frustration

He appears to be in a state of frustration and indecision (4th July) but adds,

The only consolation is that everybody is in the same boat – but that doesn't help much. The whole regiment from the Colonel downwards is as bad tempered as a crowd of bears with sore heads. It's really rather amusing to watch the Mess these days – everybody as browned off as hell. Don't worry my sweet one. I'll be coming home to you soon if I have to desert to do it.

He mentions that several Officers have left to go to various jobs but that kind of work is not for him.

Presumably, these other jobs are in Italy because he adds that he does not want to stay in,

This God forsaken country a moment longer than necessary.

At one point, Tony considers joining the Indian Civil Service.

And the proposition really did look attractive. The one snag was that my plan included living in India for a minimum of ten years – that's another reason I hadn't mentioned it to you. I didn't know how to ask you to do that. Anyhow I couldn't have decided on anything without having first talked to you. I was hoping that I would get home before anything happened. But it has happened and I've had to make a decision here and now. So I decided to play safe and stick to the army.

The latest developments here, if you can possibly call them developments, point to the probability of our remaining in this absurd state of ignorance, uncertainty and tension for several weeks. I literally daren't go back to the Foresters for fear that I shall miss the opportunity of going home with what remains of this unit. They are even talking of sending the squadrons off again on recreational training trips. M Squadron proposes to go to the Sorrento area – of all places. Don't quite know how that's going to work out as far as I'm concerned. Certainly it's a very beautiful place but full of bitter-sweet memories.

14th July

My darling wife,
Had quite a busy day today for a change. The squadron has moved again. Not very far this time – in fact only three quarters of a mile. We've gone down to our bathing cove and it really is very pleasant. Anyway, it's got us out of the dust and dirt and heat and general oppressiveness of the camp. I've got a grand site for my tent, almost on the edge of a ten-foot cliff. I've also scrounged a table and a chair and so with the addition of my bed and your photographs my home is complete.
Last night the Sergeant's Mess gave the most ginormous party. I got to bed at half-past four this morning still quite sober which I thought was no mean achievement. At half-past nine, when I dragged myself out of bed, the Quartermaster and his Sergeant were still sitting at a table with glasses of vermouth in their hands and still conscious. I shouted in the Q's ear that his store was on fire but he didn't seem to care much.
I love you more and more each day, my sweet Joy. God bless you and Josephine and keep safe. Tony

16th July

We had a unit dance last night in the local town. There's a very pleasant garden come grotto with fairy lights and all the trimmings, and on the whole I think it was a success. Womenfolk of most of the United Nations were there – Poles, Yanks, New Zealanders, South Africans and a solitary English girl (from an Indian Hospital). Of course there weren't nearly enough of them so Case withheld his irresistible charm and democratically allowed his soldiers to have the pickings.

22nd July The Swimming Gala

I've been buggering about to put it crudely. On Wednesday I had to go down to Bari to do my turn guarding the Syrian mutineers. On Thursday I came all the way back for a swimming gala in which I was an official and a competitor. Then back to Bari on guard on Friday and yesterday I was relieved. Got back in time to be taken out to dinner by my patrol – the party ended up in the sea at two o'clock in the morning.

The swimming gala was a great success. It lasted all day and there was every variety of event, serious and comic. I swam 'til I was just about dead beat and although I was only first in one event, I won over two pounds in prize money, highly satisfactory. My best performance was in the 'diving for beer' competition. Thirty bottles were sunk in fifteen feet of water. There were at least forty competitors but I ended up with three bottles to my credit which didn't go far when my patrol got hold of me.

This afternoon I played cricket for the regiment – the first time for two years.

Don't know what to say about coming home Joy my sweet. I'm just as likely to be back within a month as I am to be still out here. I just haven't got a clue.

You have all of me, Joy, forever. Tony.

Back at home, Joy anticipates that Tony will return home soon. She eagerly reads his letters and continues waiting for his safe return. Her very last letter echoes this expectancy.

Every letter that comes now I pray as I'm slitting it open that it will say 'Don't write anymore!' I shall pass out with the sheer joy of it. It seems such a long, long time since I left Italy. God bless you, my beloved husband. I pray every night for your safe return.

And so she waits.

Tony, Bari Italy 1945

Joy, Jo, Freddie, Rex, Eileen, Bertha
and Frederick 1945

Joy and Angus 2010

Postscript

Tony never did see his daughter. He saw photos or 'snaps' as he called them but never held her in his arms. He was due to return to England with Freddie but on 31st July 1945 at 1pm, he died, the day of their second anniversary. It had always been a bit of a mystery. All we knew was that it was something to do with a swimming accident but the facts were not clear.

One story was that someone fell into the water and when they did not come up again, Tony went in to save them but a mine went off.

When I was a child I asked Mum how he had died. I was told that he had done a parachute jump and that it had gone wrong and I believed that for years.

Now, the truth is known. The information was in the same box where my Mum kept his letters. A newspaper report* from the time said it was a diving accident. A letter that was sent to my Mum gives all the details. He was diving in a small bay where they always bathed and plunged to a greater depth than usual and in so doing struck his head on the sand at the bottom. When he came up he threw his head back and then realised he couldn't move his arms and legs. He shouted for

*Derby Evening Telegraph, Wednesday August 8th, 1945

help and was rescued and taken to hospital, the 98th.

They X-rayed him and found that, in layman's terms, his neck was broken. His neck was placed in a plaster. He was conscious for the next few days and, 'His courage and humour never left him.'

Even at this time he sent a message to tell Joy not to worry too much. Chris, a close friend of Joy and Tony was working in the hospital where Tony had been taken. She wrote to Joy and said he was, 'Still fully convinced up to the last moment he would get well again although he knew that his condition was so very serious. His thoughts were with you the whole time.' Then he had trouble with his breathing and lost consciousness and passed away.

Such a devastating and tragic accident. He had survived the war and all that the war had thrown at him and then to lose his life in such unfortunate circumstances. We can only imagine what it must have been like to receive such terrible news.

Years later, Josephine felt that everyone, and perhaps Tony's parents in particular, wanted to make him into a hero for her. He had served with the Central Mediterranean Forces since the end of 1942 and was wounded in the Tunisian campaign. He had also taken part in the landing at Salerno and fought during the break-through battle at Anzio. His name is read out in the Roll of Honour at Nottingham Castle. To us, what little family he has left, he will always be a hero.

His grave is at Bari, in Italy, along with thousands of other war graves.

> life is Eternal and Love is Immortal;
> and death is only a horizon;
> and a horizon is nothing save the limit of our
> sight.
> Bishop Thomas Brett

A final entry from the diary:

What started as a sort of diary to record some events, the biggest adventure of my life, became a love story. The tragic end is not the end, we will be together again.
Part of you Tony, is always with me as you said it would be, and that part of me that died with you is forever with you, until we meet again, Beloved.

The years have passed. I hardly remember the early post-war years. Perhaps I don't want to remember. I struggled to pick up the pieces, make sense of a way of life I hadn't expected. Made numerous mistakes, took forays down several blind alleys! Tried to build a normal life for my daughter who in spite of everything had grown into an adorable and lively little girl.

My Aunt describes those later years as very difficult and sad.

Mum remained at her parent's home and did manage to get various jobs. At one time she became a housekeeper to a couple who had lived in India and had been used to having servants. She did some nursing at a local hospital but never really went back to the profession. When living at her parent's home, she helped keep the accounts for her father's business.

Mum made a new life for herself but she kept all of Tony's letters. She even kept a couple in her handbag and the handbag went with her wherever she went. When I found all these letters, and there were a lot of them, they were all tied up in neat bundles with pink or white ribbon. They belong to my sister now. One day she may read them to gain a better understanding of the father that she never met. Although the war years were later tinged with such sadness, Mum claimed that they were the happiest times in her life.

Years later Mum met my own father.

"He was my knight in shining armour," she would explain. She felt that she and Josephine had been rescued. She met him at an Officers' Club. He had been in the Tank Regiment attached to the Eighth Army. He too, had served in North Africa and Italy but fortunately, had never seen any action. He had learnt to drive on the tanks so he had never taken an official driving test. There was a standing joke in our family about Dad's driving.

"Why does he drive so slowly!" some of us would exclaim. Maybe it was a reflection of his times in the Tank Regiment!

My father was very understanding about Mum's first love and he took up the challenge of bringing up my sister with sensitivity and care. After all, he was 'Dad' to her.

Mum lived a full and happy life and died at the good old age of 94. She died on the very same day as Nelson Mandela. What distinguished company to go out with, she would have liked that!

Appendix

Derby Evening Telegraph, Wednesday August 8th, 1945

Death Through Diving Mishap

Captain R.A. Case (23), son of Captain and Mrs. R. J. Case, of Derwent-avenue, Allestree, has died as a result of a diving accident while serving with the Sherwood Foresters, attached to the Special Boat Service, at Bari, in Italy.

He had been serving with the Central Mediterranean Forces since the end of 1942, and was wounded in the Tunisian Campaign.

He married Miss Joy Barber, a member of the Q.A.I.M.N.S., in Algiers, and leaves a daughter a few months old.

Captain Case took part in the landing at Salerno and also fought during the break-through battle at the Anzio beachhead.

His death occurred on July 31.

Joining the Army soon after his 19th birthday Captain Case had intended to make the Army his career.

Acknowledgements

I would like to thank my son Dave for all his hard work and my husband for his support. Thank you to John Hayter for letting me include his story and a special thanks to Uncle Freddie.
I would also like to thank Wendy for her help with the cover.

48581708R00099

Made in the USA
Charleston, SC
07 November 2015